M000307075

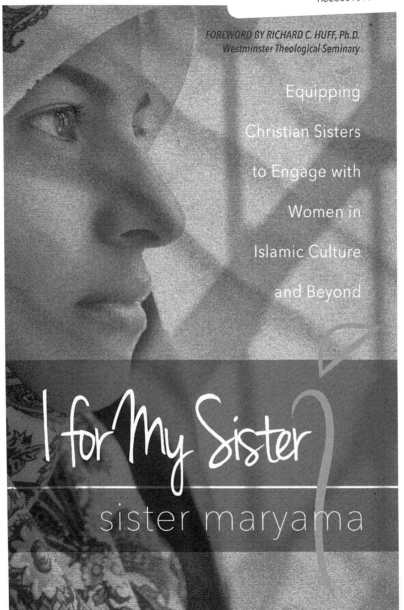

FOREWORD BY RICHARD C. HUFF, Ph.D.
Westminster Theological Seminary

Equipping

Christian Sisters

to Engage with

Women in

Islamic Culture

and Beyond

# I for My Sister?

## sister maryama

Published by Maryama Salaad Burger
California, U.S.A.

Published by Maryama Salaad Burger
California, U.S.A.

Cover design and interior layout by emdeecreative@gmail.com

Paperback ISBN: 978-0-9863166-2-3

# Dedication & Acknowledgements

THE FIRST DEDICATION with Honor and Glory goes to the lover of my soul—my Lord and savior, Jesus Christ. And to my beloved husband Ken, who is a gift from the lover of my soul, and who always has been "Jesus with skin" to me. Ken, you are the best husband, a friend and a brother and I love you dearly.

To My beautiful daughter Eda, who walks into my soul with a wooden shoes: "Eda you are my trophy of grace and I love you immensely. To my Eric: "Jesus introduced Himself to us when you were about 8 or 9 years old with your mum and sister. Your faith has survived high school, college and Law School, and life in Denmark. My heart skips a beat every time I think of what the Lord is doing in your life. To Matthew: You have come to my life such a time as this when I married your father and blessed me with two beautiful girls who call me "OMMA." We have begotten each other. To Sally and Jenny who belong to our Eric and Matthew: There are no daughters-in-law—just daughters.

To Barbara, the editor of this book, and Mark, who designed this project from cover to cover. Your contribution to this work is greatly appreciated; especially your faithfulness to the scriptures. To my best friend and dearly beloved brother, Dr Richard Huff, who wrote the forward of this book, and his beautiful wife Loretta: Your love and encouragement is immensely enjoyed.

To the Thru the Bible Radio Ministry by Dr. J. Vernon McGee, whom the Lord has used to ground me in the Word. And to my pastor, who reminds me of the mystery of grace: Pastor Brian and Cheryl, you allowed our church to be a hospital for the sick, lonely, downtrodden, and marginalized—and also for well-to-do and successful to find sweet haven for their souls in the Lord.

Finally, I thank all the many sisters and brothers who have touched and enriched my life whose names are in the book of life. I love you all.

This book is dedicated to my sweet Jesus, who is also the Lion of Judah and the Lamb who was slain from before the foundations of the world, and whose sacrifice has made a way of restoration with God and has made us joint heirs in the body of Christ. Blessings.

*In His grip,*

*Maryama*
*sistermaryama.blogspot.com*

# contents

# foreword

IF YOU PICKED UP THIS BOOK looking for an expert's opinions on missionary outreach to Muslim refugees and immigrants in the United States, you will be disappointed. The writer's strength is not sharing her views or even opening up her heart but listening to God as He shares His views and opens His heart to her. You will marvel over the clarity with which Maryama has learned to distinguish and listen loyally to God's voice!

I first met Maryama Burger at a Hospital Christian Fellowship conference in California. There is a quiet, humble intensity about Maryama that is soon impressed upon all who meet her. As she shares in her autobiographical earlier book, *From the Crescent to the Cross* (2015), Maryama spent her youth as a simple shepherdess in her homeland of Somalia. To this day she is probably most at home out in nature listening to the wind, the creatures of the wilderness, and to her Lord and God.

In her first book, Maryama recounted her journey from a life where every guiding principle of her society arose from the teachings of Islam, then through long years of personal and spiritual wandering, until she yielded to the graceful embrace of her Savior, Jesus Christ, from whom she first experienced unconditional love and forgiveness. She aches with respect and compassion for all daughters of Islam to become true daughters of Abraham by receiving the gifts of grace Abraham's God makes available through Jesus Christ alone.

Maryama is no self-appointed expert. Her writings are fragrant with the freshness of one who can still hardly believe that "my Jesus," as she tenderly calls Him, would long for her enough to go to any lengths and to pay any price necessary to set her free from sin and self and to release her to experience the joys of our Heavenly Father's arms! She never reads anything from the Bible without allowing God's Spirit to expose her own shortcomings or obstinacy in resisting His will.

As a pastor, I have been concerned that sensational news reports of violence by Islamic radicals would condition even followers of Jesus Christ to fear and avoid contact with Muslims. Last fall, I helped to organize a citywide seminar in my hometown in the Southwestern United States to help our local churches best understand how to pray for and reach out to Muslims for whom our Savior died as surely as He died for anyone. If *I for My Sister* had then been available, I would have gifted a copy to all who attended. Maryama does not offer us an encyclopedia on understanding every aspect of the life and religion of Muslims. She does offer us a practical, simplified manual on how best to view the United States through the eyes of Muslim women, especially refugees, and how best to gain their favor and their openness to the peace, security, and affirmation of their worth they will find by committing the care of their souls and their lives to Jesus.

Maryama explains why evangelism of Muslims and their discipleship as followers of Jesus is best done initially in homes rather than in our churches. Some of her insights on how to behave in a Muslim home are almost comical and point out how easily we might unknowingly offend Muslims, such as, it being impolite to finish everything on our plate and not bringing a dog (which devout Muslims believe are cursed).

Many will find Maryama's chapter on Christian Millennials the most eye-opening. She presents convincing reasons why Christian young people in the generation born in the years 1979 to 2001 have been raised up especially by God to reach out effectively to the sea of immigrants and refugees coming to the shores of America. Millennials are often willing to meet any condition to win them to Jesus.

You already have this book in your hands (or on your device). You are therefore in for a rare treat. You will find *I for My Sister* an easy read and profoundly life changing!

*Richard C. Huff*
*Ph.D. Westminster Theological Seminary*
*February, 2017*

# preface

WHEN THE LORD put it on my heart to write this book, I had no idea where it would end up. But as I stepped out in faith, it seemed the Lord took over the steering wheel and the words came without much effort; my ears and my eyes became His as I began to engage different immigrants, different congregations, different young people, who are followers of Jesus in both Christian and secular colleges.

Everywhere I went, I saw stories of redemption—and stories waiting to be redeemed. And it all started with the dialogue of an open heart and a willing spirit to hear and see the world around me with the heart and mind of Jesus. In a moment of clarity, I saw the world as "Saved"—and "Yet-to-Be-Saved." The Lord once again impressed in my heart that in order to be a witness for Him, I have to know something about the nonbeliever—spiritually, culturally and personally as well. He exposed to me many Christians in different denominations doing different ways of worship and teaching; yet the centrality of Christ was clear.

When I became a Christian out of Islam, the Lord divinely guided me into Calvary Chapel churches, where I was grounded in the Word along with the five-year, book-by-book teaching of Dr. J. Vernon McGee. Later, to my surprise, I found out that not every church was doing the same thing; and yet the Lord was there. And

He was honoring and sustaining them by what they knew and heard of Him with a tender heart of love and sweetness. I am truly blessed and continue to enjoy every one of them as "joint heirs" with Jesus!

This book is divided into two major sections:

## SECTION ONE

In Section One, we'll explore in bird's-eye view the 12 major world religions (for we are all religious and have some sort of faith in something). This will give us a chance to enhance and develop a meaningful, lasting relationship when we understand a person's core beliefs that forms their worldview. This section also exhorts us to get to know people as individuals—by understanding their culture, personality, and learning about their joy, their pain, and their dreams and aspirations.

People used to come to this country for better life and opportunity for them and their children. I was shocked when I asked a new immigrant why she came. She locked her eyes into mine and said, "PEACE—We came to have peace."

I wept.

As the Lord Jesus promised, "Peace I leave with you, My peace I give to you; not as the world gives do I give to you. Let not your heart be troubled, neither let it be afraid" (John 14:27).

This is the heart of this book.

## SECTION TWO

In Section Two, we'll survey an outline of the entire Bible. I compiled this section after I visited other churches and found out they were not fully grounded in the Word. In order to share our incredible Word of Life, we must know what we believe, and why. As a new believer, I remember how confusing and difficult it was for me to read and understand the Bible; so it is my prayer that this section will strengthen all believers, both new and growing, by creating a hunger and thirst for the Word of God.

It is my prayer and my heart's desire for this book to be a bridge builder between the Saved and Yet-to-Be-Saved. The Bible commentary is not comprehensive; rather, it is meant to give a quick survey of each book so that the Christian who is not well versed in the Bible but is filled with the Spirit can share with others. And others who are Yet-to-Be-Saved may gain a quick understanding of each book. Jesus is The Word—and the Bible is the Word of God. May you be immensely blessed in your journey of discovering Him and his purpose for you!

*In His grip,*

*Maryama Burger*
*sistermaryama.blogspot.com*

# SECTION ONE

## To Seek and To Save

# chapter one

# The Desire of My Soul

*The Desire of our soul is for Your name and for the remembrance of You.* —Isaiah 26:8

IN MY LAST BOOK, I mentioned that God was beckoning me to a new adventure. Even though I was uncertain as to exactly where He was calling me, I was confident that He would reveal His plans in due time. That is the God that I have come to know through the years—always fresh, always dynamic, always doing new things.

It was December of 2014 when our church had a women's Christmas tea. The theme was the worship of God in all the nations. Since our fellowship is blessed with many of us from different nations, we put on our different costumes. We all enjoyed appetizers from various countries, and it was beautiful. As usual, I was a shepherdess, and once again Cheryl, the head of the women's ministry, appeared, seemingly out of nowhere, asking me if I would talk about how our Christian sisters can engage the Muslim women in our midst. Suddenly it hit me. Could it be that my precious Jesus somehow wants me to be involved in writing about how the daughters of Abraham can engage the daughters of Adam—especially Muslim women?

Fear set in, because I have been there before and it did not end well. I still remember the rejection I experienced, and yet I knew that I was entering a new paradigm, and it was suddenly clear to me why He wanted me to come closer. Once again I submitted.

The workshop I held during the women's conference went well. In my first book, I had mentioned my heart's desire that someday the church would play a role in welcoming newcomers into our country and prayed that it might begin with me. It is true that the church plays an important role in helping to settle the new immigrants, because there are many logistics, and the church has a willing heart and hard-working Christian volunteers. But when the government supplies the means, there is a conflict regarding what the church agencies can do, spiritually speaking, because it is tough to bite the hand that feeds you.

This is where we fail as people of faith in giving the lost the real bread of life and the living water so that they do not have to depend on that benevolent Beast, "the government." But imagine what the results would be if independent Christian individuals, who have no connection with the government, come and befriend an immigrant! Christianity is at its best when it operates as an organism and not as an organization. I remember that the Christian organization that helped me and my family was professional and efficient, but I was unable to engage them on a spiritual level for fear of losing their support and, as a new Christian, that disappointed me.

I understand that things are not as simple as they ought to be. I know that it is not the church as an organization that can change the world but individual believers within the body of Christ, acting as an "Organism," that can change others one heart at a time. After all, is this not how our Jesus engages us—one heart at time? I am praying that the tide will soon turn and that Christian sisters will be ready to answer the call. How glorious!

So here begins a new adventure, and this time I have a troop of Christians, among which you, the reader, are a part! But Christians need to be culturally prepared in order to engage properly, and I believe that God is calling me to prepare my Christian sisters to connect with women in the Islamic culture and those in other cultures also.

As always, we have an enemy who thinks he can thwart God's perfect plan and who tends to forget who our God is. He never learns! He managed to hassle me for a while, but our God will move forward with His plans regardless.

A while ago, our church was planning to go to Israel, and though I desired to see the Holy Land, I did not think it was feasible at this time due to my husband's work schedule and his bad back as well, so I assumed that going to Israel was not for us. One Sunday, our pastor announced the upcoming trip once again and said that this was the last call to register. Suddenly, I sensed the clear voice of the Lord telling me that I needed to go to Israel. My reply was, *Lord, if this is you, and you want me to go to Israel, you have to let my husband know.* Little did I know that my precious Lord was saying the same thing to Kenny. We enjoyed the service that morning, and I kept the matter in my heart. After we came home, had sat down for our Sunday dinner, and had given thanks for our food, Kenny told me that he was going to send me to Israel! I was astonished. Why is it that we are always surprised when the Lord does something on our behalf? *O, ye of little faith!*

I had never traveled without Kenny before, and the thought of traveling alone in a foreign country was a challenge for me—not to mention that my passport states that my country of birth is Somalia. And yet I am going to Israel? Just try to imagine what might lie ahead for me. (I will return to my experience at the airport and the trip to Israel later.) I had no idea why God was sending me there, but I was filled with anticipation and excitement about what my sweet Jesus had in store for me in the land of His birth.

My trip to Israel was a little rough due to the strict airport security for those traveling to Israel. As soon as the Israeli airline staff saw my passport, a host of issues were triggered and I was pulled to one side. I was questioned, then taken to another person who asked more questions, and then I was sequestered in another area. I finally arrived at the departure gate, where I was just able to catch my breath when I was suddenly snatched away again and put in a small room. The security personnel took my purse, my shoes, and my socks, and asked more questions. I was held there till boarding time, separated from my group.

I told myself that I was specially "chosen" as I attempted to keep my sanity. After an hour, I was taken to the airplane by myself. Minutes later, the rest of the passengers joined me. My roommate was upset because she thought that I had ditched her, which opened other issues for us that almost spoiled my trip. The Lord strengthened me through all of this, and I remained calm, not even taking offense. This itself is evidence of a life that has been touched by the living God. The Israeli staff just wanted to make sure that I was not a terrorist. How could anyone know that I was in love with their Messiah and that He was beckoning me to His land if I had given in to allowing myself to feel hurt?

Once we were seated and the flight was calm, we were allowed to roam, free to talk with the staff and with each other. I had the privilege of sitting with a beautiful sister and her gracious husband from San Diego, and in front of us were two young Israeli women. One was very engaging and curious about our fascination with Israel. We told her that it is our *spiritual* birthplace and gave her a quick history lesson on God and Israel and explained why we love Israel.

It was obvious that she sensed that this was true, and she was drawn to us. She did not know that it was her Messiah who was speaking through us!

The trip was long, but I was filled with excitement and anticipation. I was especially blessed with my seatmates, and seeds of friendship, love, and sisterhood were sown. One seatmate and I made a covenant with each other to pray for the Israeli girl and her family. She was a newlywed and was on her way to visit her mother-in-law. May she find favor in her sight, like Ruth with Naomi.

We finally arrived at Galilee, where the ministry of my Jesus began. It was glorious, but sadly, my roommate situation was not as glorious. For the four nights that we were in Galilee, it seemed that I could do nothing right in her eyes, and I was truly hurt by it. Every time I thought, *Perhaps tonight will be better,* it never was. I was embarrassed and felt awkward, but I finally realized that I was in the midst of spiritual warfare, and if I failed to put to an end to this, I would have missed a great and precious opportunity of hearing what the Lord had for me. I am not sure exactly what happened next, and I am puzzled about the whole thing even now, but I knew that this sister knows and loves my Jesus and that we will have a perfect relationship in Heaven. Meanwhile, I was praying for the Holy Spirit to provide a room that would work on our behalf. After talking to my Jesus, I called my husband to let him know what was going on. As always, my husband was filled with compassion and told me to get out of there and find my own room, which I did.

The rest of my time in Israel was wonderful, and I saw many historical sites, one of which was the museum of the Holocaust. The horror of what had taken place was emotionally draining, and I found myself wishing that we could go back to the hotel and lie down for the rest of the afternoon, even though the trip was designed to help people to know and see these famous sites of our faith. I have longed to connect with the people in the land, and God honored my heart's desire. I met this Jewish young mother from San Diego with her group, the Jewish American Women's Federation, while standing in line at the Holocaust Museum. We immediately began conversing, and she told me that she had come to Israel to discover her heritage so that she could teach her children. When she asked me why I was there, I told her that I had also come in order to know my spiritual heritage, and I told her that I was a Christian and gave a quick review about their Messiah. She seemed moved by my love for the Jewish people and their Messiah "Jesus," and I mentioned His name. I continue to pray for that young Jewish mother every time she comes to mind. I remember our eyes meeting as we watched the horror that had happened as we toured the museum, with our tear-filled eyes fixed on each other, somehow trying to comprehend the depth of human depravity. I have a feeling that neither she nor I will ever be the same, because during that brief encounter, we experienced the depths of the human soul.

I have never before seen a country that is facing so much danger everyday and yet remains peaceful. I loved the way they seem to enjoy everyday life and make the best of it. They dance a lot.

We walked on Via Dolorosa, and I was saddened but grateful for all that He had done for me. We saw the empty tomb. Seeing the tomb made us sad because we realized what He had gone through for our sakes, but we realized immediately that He was not there! He is risen and alive forevermore. Glorious!

It was incredible to actually see the land of Israel, especially Jerusalem, the place where God has put His name. Out of all the places on earth, He chose *this* place. There was nothing attractive about it. Heaps of rocks and stones lay everywhere. One would think that God might have chosen a more attractive place, perhaps like Hawaii, but no! Jerusalem is the place that He has chosen for Himself. Mystery of God! Still, the question of why God had brought me here lingered in my mind.

# chapter two

# I Call Them My People

*I will call them My people, who were not My people.*
*And her beloved, who was not beloved.* —ROMANS 9:25

GOD BROKE THROUGH to me in the wilderness of Judea, hills
upon hills that seemed barren,, and yet He was there. He showed
me that He was building a foundation for a ministry and reminded
me that every time He called his people into ministry He would first
take them into the wilderness. Since I am a shepherdess, it seemed
right that He would reveal Himself in the back of the mountains. He
brought to my mind how Moses was called, and also Elijah, John
the Baptist, and He, himself—Jesus. And even though I am not any
of those great prophets and can in no way compare myself to them,
I still believe that our God calls each one of us to a specific ministry
that only we are able to do at such a time as this.

I had no idea at the time what all of this entailed, but I knew that my Jesus was on the move. After I returned from Israel, calls began coming in from people who wanted me to speak to their congregations. Suddenly, I became nervous, having a fear of public speaking, but the Lord stood by me, and I found myself becoming more comfortable every time I spoke, and I saw that people were being blessed. I am continually amazed at how each person is ministered to, how God just knows what each person needs.... God, you are so amazing!

This book is meant to engage newcomers in our country and to strengthen one another in the faith. Because I also was once a newcomer, it seemed to please my Jesus that I should be the one to write this book with a sensitive and tender heart, which has the tendency to break at times.

My Jesus gave me the name of the book and the design on the cover. The outline for the interior came as I stepped out, writing in faith.

As I see it, there are three reasons why the church needs to minister to new immigrants:

1.  God's desire for us is to be kind and hospitable to strangers. (Hebrew 13:2-3: "Do not forget to entertain strangers, for by so doing some have unwittingly entertained angels. Remember the prisoners as if chained with them—those who are mistreated—since you yourselves are in the body also.")

2.  God brought these immigrants to us because we are not always able to share His love in those countries that are hostile to the love of God, which is portrayed in the face of Jesus. (2 Peter 3:9: The Lord is not slack concerning His promise, as some count slackness, but is longsuffering toward us, not willing that any should perish but that all should come to repentance.)

3.  God loves them. He died for them and is not will-
    ing that any should perish. (John 3:16-17: For God so
    loved the world that He gave His only begotten Son,
    that whoever believes in Him should not perish but
    have everlasting life. For God did not send His Son
    into the world to condemn the world, but that the
    world through Him might be saved.)

How we engage them will depend upon their cultural background. We must also seek to understand their customs and their
spiritual needs in order to avoid any offenses. Everyone's need for
God may seem different. God's attributes get crystalized when we
are in need, much the same as when someone has been through war:
God is their shelter and safety. When someone is abused, He is their
protector. When someone is lonely, He is their companion. When one
is brokenhearted, He is their comforter, and so on. We discover the
only One who can truly meet our needs. Remember that God, who is
unchangeable, is able to do whatever He wants, but our God is a God
of mercy, tenderness, compassion, and lovingkindness, who hears
when we cry out to Him. God views each of us individually. And
this is what we are going to explore in this book. It will require love,
prayer, and patience on our parts. So let us begin.

## A BRIEF DESCRIPTION OF THE RELIGIONS OF THE WORLD

The information that I am about to share is general knowledge
that can be found in many books or on the Internet. It is intended to
provide a short introduction to the major world religions. The site
from which I mostly gleaned from is called infoplease.com. There are
12 classical world religions that we will explore, but I am sure there

are many more. On these pages I will simply state the fundamental core belief of each religion, so please pay close attention to what I am about to share. When you better understand someone's beliefs or religion or cultural bent, it tells them that you care about them and would like to know more about them. "For God so loved the world that He gave His only begotten Son, that whosoever believes in Him should not perish but have everlasting life."

Imagine that! God loved us enough to die for us! I do not understand it either. That mystery is reserved for Him.

The following are the major world religions:

**Hinduism**

The origins of Hinduism can be traced to the Indus Valley civilization sometime between 4000 to 2500 BC. This people group is believed to follow a polytheistic religion, which means a belief in many gods. The basis of Hinduism is the belief in the unity of *everything*. This totality is called Brahman, also known as the "final cause of all that exists" [https://en.wikipedia.org/wiki/Brahman]. According to their understanding, the purpose of life is to realize that we are part of God, and thus, we can leave this plane of existence and rejoin God. This experience can be achieved only by going through cycles of birth, life, and death, and is known as Samsara, a Sanskrit word meaning "wandering" or "world," and indicates a "cyclic, circuitous change" [https://en.wikipedia.org/wiki/Samsara]. One moves toward "enlightenment," the progress of which is measured by one's "karma." This is the accumulation of all one's good and bad deeds, thus determining the person's next reincarnation. Selflessness in thoughts and actions along with devotion to God results in one's rebirth to a higher level. On the other hand, bad actions, and even bad thoughts, will cause one come back after death at a lower level, whether human or possibly even as an animal.

Most Hindus follow a strict caste system, which determines the standing of each person. The caste: only the members of the highest caste, the Brahmins, may perform religious rituals and certain other vital religious tasks within the temples [https://www.britannica.com/topic/Brahman-caste].

## Confucianism

The founder is K'ung-fu-tzu, who was born about 551 BC in the state of Lu in China. "China's most famous teacher, philosopher, and political theorist," his "ideas have influenced the civilization of Asia" [https://www.britannica.com/biography/Confucius]. He traveled throughout China giving advice to its rulers and teaching them. His teachings primarily dealt with individual morality and ethics along with the proper exercise of political power. The Five Constants are:

1. Ren (benevolence, humaneness)
2. Yi (righteousness or justice)
3. Li (proper rite [principle of gain, benefit, order, propriety])
4. Zhi (knowledge)
5. Xin (integrity) [https://en.wikipedia.org/wiki/Confucianism#Ethics]

Unlike most religions, Confucianism is primarily an ethical human-centered system with rituals for certain times during one's lifetime. The most important periods recognized in the tradition of Confucianism are birth, reaching maturity, marriage, and death. Thus, Confucianism is essentially a system that offers instructions for how to live right and do good.

## Buddhism (560 to 490 BC)

Buddhism developed out of the teachings of Siddhartha Gautama who in 535 BC reached enlightenment and assumed the title Buddha. He promoted the "middle way as the path of enlight-enment rather than the extremes of mortification of the flesh or worshiping the flesh." Long after his death, the Buddha's teaching were written down.

Buddhism promotes belief in reincarnation and that one must go through numerous cycles of birth, life, and death. After many such cycles, if a person releases their attachment to desire and the self, he may attain Nirvana. In general, Buddhists do not believe in any type of deity, the need for a savior, prayer, or eternal life after death. Today's Buddhism, however, has nevertheless integrated many religious rituals, beliefs, and customs, and, because of its "flu-idity" and its philosophical nature, it encounters little or no conflict even in the West.

**Shintoism (500 + BC)**

This is an ancient Japanese religion that is recognized unoffi-cially as the national religion of Japan and has close ties to nature, believing in the existence of various "kami," or nature spirits. It is not a philosophy as much as a ritualistic religion that sees human beings as essentially "good." Its followers desire peace and have no teach-ings on original sin or of fallen man. They believe that all human life is sacred, and sincerity and morality are encouraged as long as they benefit the group. Among their teachings, the main ones are:

1. Tradition and family
2. Love of nature, which is sacred, and natural objects are to be worshiped as sacred spirits.
3. Physical cleanliness through bathing, hand washing, and rinsing of the mouth.
4. Love of nature, with nature being understood as sacred and natural objects are to be worshiped as spirits.

5.  The Matsuri Festival, which honors the spirits, is also part of the practice.

## Sikhism (1500 BC)

One of the major world religions, Sikhism was founded by Sri Guru Nanak Dev Ji in the Punjab area now in Pakistan. "The faith system is based on the teachings of Guru Nanak Dev and ten successive Sikh Gurus, with the last one being revealed in sacred scripture, Guru Granth Sahib" (www.sikhiwiki.org/index.php/Sikhism).

Sikhs believe in a single formless God with many names, who is the Universal God. Salvation can be earned by disciplined, personal meditation on the name and message of God, who can be known through that meditation. Sikhs pray many times a day and prohibit the worship of idols or icons.

They believe in Samsara, karma, and reincarnation, as Hindus do, but they reject the caste system of Hinduism. According to Sikhism, everyone has equal status in the eyes of God.

## Zoroastrianism (1000 BC)

"The ancient pre-Islamic religion of Iran (formerly Persia)... founded by the Iranian prophet and reformer Zoroaster in the 6th century BC" ... In more recent times the study of Zoroastrianism has played a decisive part in reconstructing the religion and social structure of the Indo-European peoples (https://www.britannica.com/topic/Zoroastrianism).

They dedicate their lives to a three-fold path represented by their motto: a) good thoughts; b) good words; c) good deeds.

## Judaism (2000 BC)

Judaism, Christianity, Islam, and the Baha'i faith all originated with a divine covenant between one true God and His friend Abraham, and while the similarities somewhat end there, with the exception of Christianity, which accepts the Torah (the Old Testament) as part of the Christian Bible) the Jews in general do not accept the New Testament, nor do they believe that Jesus is the Messiah.

The next leader of the Israelites, Moses, led his people out of Egypt and received the law from God. Joshua later led them into the Promised Land, where the prophet Samuel established the Israelite kingdom with Saul as its first king. King David established Jerusalem, and King Solomon built the first temple.

In 70 AD, the temple was destroyed and the Jews were scattered throughout the world until 1948 when the state of Israel was formed.

Jews believe in one Creator, who alone is to be worshiped as absolute ruler of the universe. He monitors people's activities, and He rewards good deeds and punishes evil.

The Torah was revealed to Moses by God and cannot be changed. Though God does communicate with the Jewish people through the prophets, the Jews believe in the inherent goodness of the world and its inhabitants as creations of God and do not believe that a Savior is necessary to save them from original sin. They believe that they are God's chosen people and that the Messiah will arrive in the future, gather them into Israel, there will be a general resurrection of the dead and the temple that was destroyed in 70 AD will be rebuilt.

## Baha'i' (1863 AD)

The Baha'i faith arose from Islam in the 1800s, based on the teachings of Baha'u'llah, and is now a distinct worldwide faith. It is one of the youngest faiths known at this time.

The faith's followers believe that God has sent nine great prophets to mankind through whom the Holy Spirit has revealed the Word of God. This has given rise to major religions.

The Baha'i' religion believes that each prophet revealed his message due to the needs of the society that they had come to help and what mankind was ready to have revealed to it.

The faith promotes gender and race equality, freedom of expression and assembly, world peace, and world government. Led by Baha'is, this government will be established at some point in the future. The faith does not attempt to preserve the past but does embrace the findings of science. Baha'is believe that every person has an immortal soul that cannot die but that is free to travel through the spirit world after death.

## Jainism (420 BC)

Like Hinduism and Buddhism, Jainism came from the same part of the world, and its followers believe in Karma and reincarnation. They believe that enlightenment can be achieved through asceticism. They also believe in fruitarianism, the practice of only eating that which will not kill the plant or animal from which it is taken.

Another practice is *ahimsa*—non-violence—because any act of violence against a living thing creates negative Karma, which will adversely affect one's next life.

## Taoism (440 AD)

Tao, roughly translated as "path," is a force that flows through all life and is the first cause of everything. The goal of everyone is to become one with Taoist Tai

Chi, a technique of exercise using slow deliberate movements, which is used to balance the flow of energy, or chi, within the body. People should develop virtue and seek compassion, moderation, and humility. One should plan any action in advance and achieve it through minimal action.

*Yin* (the dark side) and *yang* (the light side) symbolize pairs of opposites, which are seen throughout the universe, such as good and evil, light and dark, male and female.

The impact of human civilization upsets the balance of yin and yang. Taoists believe that people are by nature good and that one should be kind to others simply because such treatment will probably be reciprocated.

### Islam (622 AD)

Islam was founded in 622 AD by the prophet Muhammad in Mecca, which today is considered the most sacred place in Islam, and to which millions of Muslims make their yearly pilgrimage.

Though it is one of the youngest of the world's great religions, Muslims do not view it as a new religion. They believe that it is the same faith taught by the prophets Abraham, David, Moses, and Jesus. The role of Muhammad as the last prophet was to formalize and clarify the faith and purify it by removing ideas that were added in error.

The two sacred texts of Islam are the Qur'an, which consists of the words of Allah, whom they consider to be the one true God, as given to Muhammad through visions and dreams, and the Hadith, which is a collection of Muhammad's sayings.

The duties of all Muslims are known as the five pillars of Islam:

1.  Recite the *shahadah* at least once. The Shahadah, in Arabic, states,"I bear a witness that Allah is one god and I bear a witness that prophet Mohamed is his only prophet." This is the most important pillar of the five, for it is the first acknowledgment or admittance to the Muslim faith.

2.  Perform the salat ( prayer) 5 times a day, facing the Ka'aba in Mecca.

3.  Give alms to charity—about 2.5 percent of your substance.

4. Fasting during the month of Ramadan from dawn to dusk. (The month during which Muhammad received the Qur'an from Allah.)

5. Make the pilgrimage to Mecca at least once in lifetime, if economically and physically able.

Muslims follow strict monotheism with one creator, who is just, omnipotent, and merciful. They all believe in Satan, who drives people to sin, and they believe that all unbelievers and sinners will spend eternity in hell. Muslims who sincerely repent and submit to God will return to a state of sinlessness and go to paradise after death. They adhere to moral laws, and alcohol, drugs, and gambling are prohibited. They reject racism.

They respect the earlier prophets, Abraham, Moses, and Jesus, but they regard the concept of the deity of Jesus blasphemous and do not believe that He was executed on the cross.

They also believe that one day the world will be under the subjection of Islam, and that God has rejected the Jewish people. Even though Islam traces its foundations to Abraham, and there are many similarities in the Old Testament and in some of the new, these traditions in the everyday life of Jews and Muslims, food, marriage, or marriage arrangements, family, and many other traditional and cultural celebrations are very similar, although they would never admit it to one another. Nevertheless, there is a great deal of discrepancy between the god whom Muslims worship and the God of the Bible. Jews have a half revelation of God, but what they have is mostly correct. Most Muslims do not understand the Qur'an because it is written in classical Arabic, and, as far as I know, cannot be translated to another language. Since Muslims came from different continents and countries, with different languages, each group depends on their elders to interpret the Qur'an. The largest Muslim population is in Asia, and perhaps the second is in Africa. The Middle Eastern countries are the third, I believe. So their ethnicity will depend on what continent or country they come from. Some are brown, black, or white, as in central and eastern Europe. To engage them will depend on understanding their cultural background.

**Conclusion:**

There are many other belief systems, but these are the main ones to which the majority of the world adheres. Mormons (also known as "Latter Day Saints") and Jehovah's Witnesses are among many heretical (unbiblical) sects of Christianity.

All the world religions, while they differ slightly in their methodology of knowing God, seem to have three core beliefs in common:

1.  They deny the deity of Jesus Christ and that He is the Son of God.
2.  They believe that they can come to God on their own merit through their deeds, rituals, traditions, and ancestral practices or worship.
3.  They believe that man is inherently good and that all are trying to reach God through their goodness.

It is important to note that all other religions are about man trying to reach God, but Christianity is about God, who reached down to man.

# CHRISTIANITY—A LEAGUE OF ITS OWN

Even though Judaism and Islam trace their heritage to the Abrahamic faith in one God who is the Creator of heaven and earth and everything in it, like Christianity, the similarity ends there. Judaism and Islam know of God and have heard of Him but do not know the true God, who is the dynamic, true and living God, who longs to reveal Himself to everyone who desires to know Him and have an intimate relationship with Him. He is love personified, for He created man to love God and to enjoy Him forever. When we deviate from that purpose, we open ourselves to chaos and confusion.

Christianity beautifully portrays this unique relationship between a man who desires God and the God who is willing. It is not a set of rules and rituals but a state of being. We are connected to and continuously balanced and replenished by the true living God who created us for Himself and who says, "You are the apple of my eye."

The truly Christian life is an unmovable, undisturbed life that can honestly say, "All is well with my soul" when the world is unraveling around the edges. It is about a person whose name is JESUS, the author and finisher of our faith (Hebrews 12:2). And as we live in a disturbed, broken, unbalanced world, those who are in Christ are in a state of homeostasis—a state of balance, sustained by an invisible Person whose name is JESUS. Thus we can endure hardships, losses, grief, poverty, persecution, and all the ills life brings to us. We can truly say that we are more than conquerors (Romans 8:37).

Before I encountered Jesus, I consisted of body, soul, and spirit. My body was in control and obeyed its needs, wants, and desires. My soul was led by my ego and was full of pride, envy, war with self and others, greed, covetousness, with the spirit of comparison and competition. My true spirit was dormant, with no power or strength to overcome evil or to do good, and this is why the Islamic religion, which I tried to practice, has failed me, because religion always tells you to do good, but it does not give you the power to do so.

This is where Christianity shines. Not only does it tell you to do good, but it actually gives you the power and the ability to do so. This is because when you become a Christian, you enter into a relationship with the true and living God, and He resides with you and does amazing things through you. You can converse with Him. Remember, before I was merely body, soul, and spirit, but when I cried out to God, He heard me and invaded my life. All of a sudden, an inversion took place, and I became spirit, soul, and body. The Spirit became the driving force of my life. He took control of my soul and body. I became a new creation. Everything I was before is now a contradiction and strange to this new life. What I am now is contrary to everything this world expects or requires of me, and so it is with everyone who receives Jesus. He changes you from inside out, and when our innermost being is changed, then our actions and behavior reflect the change within. And the world wonders...

This new life provides humility instead pride, love instead of war, mercy instead of vengeance. It encourages me to give instead of getting, to love instead of seeking love. We are forgiven so that we can forgive, healed so that we can heal others through the love of Jesus. We are restored to God so that we can restore others. This resurrected life is the life of a true Christian who puts his trust in Christ alone. No deeds, no rituals, just Jesus. He gave His life so that we can have Him. Salvation is about losing self for others. We freely give because we freely have received. It is a spirit-operated life, full of hope and adventure. It is about God's love for us and our love for others through Him. It is indeed a life of awe and wonder. All other religions worship, praise, and sacrifice to their gods, but they cannot have a dialog or conversation with them. Only the Christian faith offers this amazing privilege.

# chapter three

# Daughters of Abraham Seeking Daughters of Adam

*How beautiful are the feet of those who preach the Gospel of Peace, who bring glad tidings of good things...* —ROMANS 10:15

EVEN THOUGH this subject includes all people who do not know our God, the focus on this book is mainly on Muslims, especially women, since they are the ones most of us seem to encounter lately, but it can apply to anyone who does not know our Jesus and whom I shall refer to as "daughters of Adam."

Daughters of Abraham are those of us who have seen and tasted the grace and the goodness of God through the Lord Jesus Christ and know that we are not dependent on our own merits to belong to God. We do not become daughters of Abraham by a physical birth but by a spiritual one. This is why we call ourselves "born again." These daughters come from all walks of life, have all different shades of skin and different backgrounds, come from different countries and cultures, and may be all ages and from religions that once had roots in the "I can come to God based on my own works and morals" philosophy. But when the time was right, at a particular moment of our lives, God shined His light into our hearts and enlightened our minds to show us the truth about Himself. Each one of us has our own beautiful story of Redemption. These stories include memories of failures, losses, pain, destruction, and feelings of inadequacy. Yet we all had one thing in common: lives that were unfulfilling; lives without meaning and purpose; lives without peace. And all because ours were lives without God.

Some of us are new immigrants and some are daughters of immigrants, but we were all daughters of Adam at one time before we came to faith through Jesus. Now we are yearning for many others who are currently daughters of Adam to become daughters of Abraham through our love, prayers, and patience.

Daughters of Adam do not receive us well, and we are often rejected, insulted, and at times persecuted by them. But we have a strong foundation and a new identity impressed upon us, and that is the Image of the living God, given to us by our sweet Savior through His blood. We each now wear a beautiful, well-fitting regal robe of righteousness. And so we press on, knowing that we are not alone, because we have our beloved Jesus in us, around us, and over us! He is our High Priest, who has gone before us and suffered much more than anyone can imagine, as is clearly stated in John 15:18-21:

> If the world hates you, you know that it hated Me before it hated you. If you were of the world, the world would love its own. Yet because you are not of the world, but I chose you out of the world, therefore the world hates you. Remember the word that I said to you, 'A servant is not greater than his master.' If they persecuted Me, they will also persecute you....But all these things

they will do to you for My name's sake, because they do not know Him who sent Me.

Jesus is our great example, who paid the ultimate price for us on the cross. And think about this: He is the one who is working through us!

Immigrant women who come to our country—those "daughters of Adam"—come with a lot of pain, brokenness, losses, and loneliness. They face many difficult issues: the loss of their country and their culture, tremendous grief over the loss of loved ones; and some may suffer Post-Traumatic Stress Disorder. They also have a tendency to suffer from identity crises and feelings of not belonging. As daughters of Abraham (Christians), we have a great opportunity to show God's love to them and to listen to their stories. This may well be the first step toward engaging them and then actually loving them.

As we reveal Jesus and listen to their stories, letting them share their wounds and brokenness with us, we are indeed ministering to them! We are cultivating the ground and actually building a foundation upon which we may some day be able to share the good news of the Gospel. When we begin to understand their culture and their foundational beliefs, we can assure them that they are valued, respected, and loved, thus promoting connection and bringing down the walls that separate us. As we get to know them better, we find that we have a greater chance of understanding their spiritual needs. Someone once said, "Nobody cares how much you know unless they know how much you care." When you are caring and loving these women, you gain credibility with them and are establishing trust when they realize that you really do care.

Prayer, love, and patience pave the way to bring them into the fold, as we never forget that we were once just like them, in darkness and without hope. I weep when I hear what they have gone through, and my sisters weep with me. Many daughters of Abraham yearn for the daughters-of-Abraham-to-be. These daughters of Adam are seeking a place and a nation where they may belong. They desire to have their identity restored—not as it was before but to something much better. Most of them have grown up in a culture where men are considered more important than women. They want to know that they, too, are respected, because here in America women appear to have more value. Even though that may be true in some respects, these immigrant women face the danger of becoming confused about who they are as women. American culture encourages women to be like men and do what men can do. In fact, women can do much of what men can do—in some cases, even more— yet these immigrant women would prefer to keep their feminine mystique. They already know who they are as women and that they are stronger and more resilient than men. Because they have grown up in a land of oppression, they are great negotiators and diplomats. They just want to not be abused, and, at the very least, they want to know that if they are abused they will be offered support and protection. This is why America is so attractive to them.

As they begin to understand these things, the American daughters of Abraham can be, and will be, a great asset to our sisters-to-be. We must educate them in the culture, teaching them that what they see in our television shows and advertisements is not true in most American lives and homes. In fact, we have more in common with them regarding our beliefs and values, and our culture is not as depraved as what they see on television or the Internet. But most of all, we must warn them of the dangers of radical feminism, which actually is a great destroyer of our culture.

We must let them see our lives, so that they might come to understand that our Jesus is pouring Himself into us, so that He can pour out from us into them! In other words, we are the vessels that contain the King of the universe, who is also our precious, loving Savior.

It's also important that we realize how much they have to teach us, if we are willing to learn from them. They love and take good care of their families, and they manage their homes well. They love to cook healthy foods, and they are great hostesses.

Most of them have some ideas and beliefs about God and His judgment, which is bad news for those who are coming to Him on their own merit. But we have the Good News of knowing the true and living God, and we have an intimate personal relationship with Him. Oh, if the world could only know! The God who says, "I am the light of the world. He who follows Me shall not walk in darkness…. Whoever drinks of the water that I shall give him will never thirst…." Again, He says, "I am the Bread of life. He who comes to Me will never hunger…" He also says: "Come to me all you who are labored and heavy laden and I will give you rest…" (John 8:12; 4:10-14; Matthew 11:28).

This is the God who is yearning to impart to us His very life so that we can have the life He created us to have: and that is eternal life with Him!

They already know the bad news. Let's tell them the Good News! Let's tell them about THE GOD WHO YEARNS FOR THEM.

**Getting to Know Our Sisters**

Cultivating personal relationships with our sisters is going to take time, prayers, and love. First, we must learn about their beliefs, their culture, and their values. Then we should get to know them personally: their history, their family, their personality, and their bents. The beauty of this is: IT IS NOT SCRIPTED! It simply means that we begin to have normal, everyday relationships: having lunch together, taking a walk, sharing afternoon tea, dinner, standing in line together, saying hello, exchanging smiles—the list is endless, because whether we are aware of it or not, we are always communicating verbally or with our body language.

Everybody likes to be affirmed with love and acceptance. After you say hello with a smile, find something beautiful about her (and do it honestly, because you are looking at her through the eyes of our Jesus): her smile, her beautiful fluid brown eyes that show her zest for life, her scarf, etc.

Now remember, this is sister to sister. After that first encounter, leave her with something that has eternal value, such as "God is pleased to have created you and is blessing you today." Remember, these women tend to be deep and poetic. But always, always make sure that you are depending on the Holy Spirit to guide you. Talk about what you have in common, or about their everyday life. *Is all well with you? or How are you? or Is everything ok with you?, How are the children or the family?* These are the things they are used to hearing. Once again, let them see the heart of Jesus in you. It isn't complicated, actually. Always ask them if you can pray for them, and affirm that you are a Christian and that you pray in the name of Jesus. If they object, it's okay. Just keep them in your prayers. We have the privilege of talking to our God. They don't have to know that we are praying for them if they aren't open to that yet. But continue the relationship, and at the same time, always be true and faithful in your relationship with your Jesus. And remember: prayer, patience and love....

**After You Have a Chance to Know Them Better—What Then?**

Ask the Holy Spirit to be your guide. Talk about the beauty of God, His Mercy, His Love. This is huge with the daughters of Adam, because they know that God exists and is the Judge of all. They know that He has standards, and those standards come under the heavy hand of the law, whether it is Moses' law or the moral law that is somehow written in every man's heart. In their mind, everybody wants to do good, no matter who they are or what they believe, by obeying the law—but there is a problem, because the law is Holy and only a Holy God is capable of keeping it. Everyone else fails. So the Law that was meant to save us actually killed every one of us. The Bible says the Law is good, if we can keep it. The law can identify our flaws, but it cannot correct those flaws.

Every daughter of Adam knows that something is terribly wrong and desires to do good. But how? Talk about God's love for them and that God *knows* our inability to keep the Law, and He has already done something about it! Tell them that "God so loved the world that He gave His only begotten Son, that whoever believes in Him should not perish but have everlasting life. For God did not send His Son to condemn the world, but that the world through Him might be saved" (John 3:16-17). This is a powerful verse for a woman to hear, because we feel pain, love, and beauty at a deep, emotional level. Tell her the story of the Cross, and let her hear the deep agony He went through. Tell her that He left everything in order to have her. It is a very compelling story and, indeed, impossible to ignore. As the Holy Spirit guides you, do not minimize the Cross. Simply tell the story. Talk about how we are guilty and could never be perfect in the eyes of a Holy God, for they do understand that God is Holy.

Share what God means to you and what He has done in your life—not in great detail yet. You might risk making them think that maybe they aren't as bad as you and thus their good behavior is enough. Remember—to them everything is from outside, whereas for us, it is inside out. So everything looks good from outside—Oh, but the heart! That is why it is so important to connect with the daughters of Adam on a deep personal level.

In the previous paragraphs I showed how you can build a relationship with her. Imagine a world in which every daughter of Abraham gets to know, in a personal way, one daughter of Adam. We would turn the world right side up!

Always keep your conversation centered on God, and if it meanders and spills over onto different subjects, do not be surprised,

There are many reasons why she may allow that to happen: fear of leaving what is familiar, and much more. We will discuss the reasons latter, but for now, gently lead her back to the subject at hand, and if you encounter resistance, simply make a gracious exit from the subject. There will be another opportunity. Do not be discouraged. Be patient, and continue the friendship, always remembering how patient our Lord is with us. Know, too, that not everybody in this world is going to be saved, but the beauty is that we do not know who, so we can see all of the world as "saved" and "yet to be saved." I am thankful that God did not share that information with us. He is so wonderful. He reserved that right for Himself. So since we do not know who will be saved, we have an awesome opportunity to share this amazing good news!

Most cultures love to give gifts, so accept any present with gratitude and wait a while before you return the favor, or she might think that she gave the impression that she wanted something in return. Giving gifts in this culture is sacred and from the heart. It conveys that you value the person, so accept the meal or gift with a grateful heart.

Take works out of the equation, because that only brings these daughters back to the law where they are stumbled. Those involved are usually moral people from outside, so go deeper, into the issues of the heart. Ask her if she feels anger, bitterness, hate, vengeance, unforgiveness, covetousness, and the like (any of the issues of the heart). Then ask, "Do you think God sees or knows your thoughts? These are the things in your heart that no one else sees."

Remember now, you know each other well by this time, and it is safe to speak openly. Next, remember what our Lord said in Mark 13:11 and follow His instructions: "But when they arrest you and deliver you up, do not worry beforehand, or premeditate what you will speak. But whatever is given you in that hour, speak that; for it is not you who speak, but the Holy Spirit."

It is common in the Islamic culture for women to have a party without men. It is more relaxing and open. They can kick their shoes off and remove their scarves or Hijabs in the comfort of the home. If you are hosting the party, make sure that the men in your home have other things to do for the day and will not be around. Learn to have fun with these ladies. Ask one to teach you how to cook her food, like hummus, tabouli, sambos, different sauces and spices. Dancing is always fun. Ask her to teach you how to wear scarves and much more.

# chapter four

# Journey of a Sister-to-Be

*For I know the thoughts that I think toward you, says the LORD,*
*thoughts of peace and not of evil, to give you a future and a hope.*
— JEREMIAH **29:11**

IN THE LAST CHAPTER, I mentioned briefly why a sister-to-be
might avoid the subject of God, and even though there are many possible reasons, especially when it comes to immigrant women, they all
come down to this one: *fear.*

- Fear of leaving what is familiar.
- Fear of being cursed if they leave their god.
- Fear of being disowned, losing family, country, culture.

The immigrant woman knows that she will lose everything she
has ever known. In some religions, she faces the very real fear of losing her life or bringing shame to her family.

These are the issues that immigrant women face. The decision is a costly one, so it is very important for the Christian sister to have much empathy and understanding and to be able to wait patiently. When she does come to Jesus—once she crosses that threshold—she will become an amazing woman of God, because she knows that her decision to follow Christ has cost her something valuable. She will also find that this is the greatest treasure that she will ever receive because she understands that her beloved Savior also left everything so that He could have her. Then she will embrace Him and come to the place where she also is willing to leave everything behind so that she can have Him, the Pearl of Great Price (Matthew 13:45-46). Both she and Jesus have found the pearl of great price—one another! For the first time in her life, the need to belong, the desire for acceptance and completeness, are fulfilled in Jesus. These three basic needs are what every woman longs for, and the answer is hidden in Jesus! This indeed has been my case, and now I can truly sing, "You can have the whole world;…just give me Jesus…."

This newly redeemed woman finds out that Jesus Christ is the one she has longed for all her life, and as she grows and develops in the Spirit, she will realize that He is enough. As He gives new life to her, she is healed, comforted, and sustained by the Lover of her soul. She learns that in His life and hers, there is much in common. He is a shepherd, He is a farmer, He is a great poet, He tells stories that bring the truth home and move the human heart, and she will realize that no man has ever spoken like Him. He, too, walked in the soil and wore sandals. His feet got dirty, like hers. He sat on rocks. He ate with His hands and reclined, as in her culture. She will also see that He is familiar with her pain and knows all about it. As she looks back at her life, she will see that He has always been with her.

Looking back, I see how He was always with me! And, like me, she will sing the song that I heard: "At the foot of the cross, now I can trade these ashes in for beauty and wear forgiveness like a crown.

Come to kiss the feet of Mercy and lay every burden down… You won my heart, sweet Jesus…."

## God Pursues Them according to Their Need

Some come to faith in Christ due to fear of death and the desire for the assurance of salvation, much like one Muslim woman, who said, "I have confidence concerning the end of my life."

As for me, I also came to Him out of fear of His judgment, because something deep within told me that all was not well with me and God, and I had felt guilty ever since my grandmother told me that God judges our hearts. That was when I lost all hope. One day, I cried out to Him, and He heard me. I did not ask for health, wealth, or an easy life. To be honest, I did not expect Him to do any of those things for me. I simply wanted to avoid going to hell. I thought I could fend for myself. I did not know that having a relationship with God was what it meant to be Christian, for He was too great and holy to have fellowship with me or with anyone else. To be forgiven was simply enough for me.

Then, as I studied the Scriptures, I realized the reality of the living God—the weight of the glory of His inexpressible love, mercy and grace. And I found myself falling in love with Him. So now, instead of coming to Him out of fear, I come to Him because I *love* Him and enjoy His presence. Our God wants to be enjoyed. In so doing, we bless Him, and we are blessed by Him. It is a glorious life!

Some come to Jesus because His character is overwhelmingly beautiful. They are amazed at His humility; as someone stated, "He never retaliated or defended Himself." He spoke not a word in His own defense. His willingness to die in another's place speaks even to other faiths. We know that a king's subjects would die for him. Oh, but a king who would die for his subjects—now *that* is moving! The Islamic religion believes there was no fault in Jesus. That means

He was sinless. And although Mohammed asked for forgiveness, the Qu'ran never mentions Jesus asking for forgiveness.

- Some people of other faiths come to Jesus through reading the Bible. They find it logical, reasonable, and sane. It is relevant and not culture bound—i.e., it makes sense.

- Some find the Bible to be intellectually agreeable as it explains the character of God.

- Some find that the Bible answers those nagging questions pertaining to all of the issues of life. It's like having the blueprint for how to live.

- Some people come to know Christ because of the love we Christians have for God and for each other as brothers and sisters in the Lord…. The Cross comes into view and is displayed in our lives.

- Some others come to Christ through visions and dreams in which Jesus actually appears to them. Here are two categories:

*Preparatory*

Someone once commented about a certain believer's immense peace and asked what her secret was, to which the believer simply stated, "Jesus." When the seeker asked what she meant, she replied, "I am a Christian." Then the woman asked how she could know which one is the right—Jesus or Mohammed. The believer's reply rocked her world. She said, "Ask God. And ask Him with a sincere heart." She promised that she would. That night before she went to bed she told God that she was searching for the truth of how to worship Him and asked, "Which one is right, Mohammed or Jesus?" She went to sleep and had a dream. In her dream she saw a multitude of people running and asked what was happening. They told her that there was a huge tsunami coming that was going to swallow the whole earth! Everyone was running to higher ground, but the waves reached to the heavens. Just when it was about to swallow the whole earth, she uttered the name *Jesus*, and she saw a huge hand stretched out over the waves, and all of a sudden, the waves stopped. She woke up, covered with sweat, and gave her life to JESUS.

*Protective*

At other times Jesus speaks to someone who is a believer to empower and strengthen him or her when they are in danger, and to give a fitting word. For example, in my case, my family and relatives were trying to persuade me to relent from my madness of being a Christian. I remember being mocked and laughed at regarding the absurdity of Christianity and hearing them baiting me to explain the Trinity, and I could not, even though I knew. They asked me how God could have a son or have a relationship with a woman. The questions kept coming, and doubt filled my mind. At that very moment, I heard the clear voice of my Jesus telling me to leave—to get out of there immediately! My Jesus rescued me that day from the mouth of the enemy. Some encounter Jesus through reading the Qur'an or the Bible or simply by coming to the Cross, as in my case.

In this relatively brief look at what God is doing within a very large cross section of humanity, we see His heart being revealed in dramatic ways. Christ extends His hand to every daughter of Adam in a way no less sincere than His hand has been extended to you and me. Many are seeking the true, living God, so let us reveal Jesus through the Cross. Sincerity of heart is a critical foundation for a life of saving faith in Christ Jesus. For our Lord said, *"You will seek me and find me when you search for me with all your heart"* (Jeremiah 29:13).

You can reveal Jesus by sharing who He is—His life story. Talk to others about how He is different from the other prophets. They will have heard about the "immaculate conception." In truth, the baby Jesus was placed into the womb of Mary in a miraculous way. They will also have heard how the prophets talked about His coming, from the ancient scriptures, and they saw the miracles He performed. No other prophet has these qualities.

Women usually do not like to debate, so as you reach out to this one, tell her about Jesus and the Cross, in a tender, loving manner in the Spirit.

The Trinity is a difficult subject to comprehend, so perhaps it is wise to wait a while unless the Holy Spirit prompts you to share, and by then He will have no doubt told you what to say. John 3:16-17 is a powerful truth to show that our God is not a condemning God but a loving Father who desires for all people to be saved. Tell her about His long- suffering and how He patiently waits for us and even helps us to come to Him. Remind her that no sin is ever so big that He will not forgive it. Pray for her to desire Him.

It is important to know and understand her culture and religion. Thus it is good to refresh your mind regarding the religions of the world that I touched on in chapter 2.

Always pray, and ask Jesus to guide, for He is willing.

A few things to remember when entering her home:

1.  Dress modestly—wearing a scarf is a plus. It shows that you value her way of life and also that you are conveying to her that you are free to wear a scarf.

2.  Most homes are shoeless. You will see shoes at the door, so do likewise and remove yours.

3.  Kissing both sides of the cheeks is customary.

4.  Accept what is offered graciously, and receive it with your right hand or with both hands. Washing your hands is always a good way to connect with them,

since they are ritualistic in nature, and it is common for them to eat with their hands.

5. Try not to finish everything on your plate. It is impolite.

6. If you encounter a male in the house, you do not need to shake hands with him. A simple hello is enough, and perhaps this would be a good time to cover your head with your scarf.

7. If you have your Bible, never, ever put it down on the floor. It shows a lack of awe and respect for the Word of God. I once heard about a young missionary who was travelling in a Muslim country and was reading his Bible in the bus. He was asked what he was reading, and he replied, "The Bible," and then he began to explain in detail that it was the Word of God. The people around him listened intently. Afterward, he put the Bible in his bag and sat on it. I heard that it was the beginning and end of his mission in that particular community. It was offensive for him to sit on the bag the Bible was in. Little things can hurt your testimony.

8. Let your light shine, be yourself, and remember that you are sharing our Jesus. The burden is on Him, and He does not mind carrying it.

9. Most of all, please examine who Jesus is in your own life. Is He enough? You can rely on the sufficiency of Christ and Him alone. Our Lord is the best, so let us showcase Him in our lives through joyful and thankful hearts. Be kind, and reveal faith, hope, and peace, which is Christ in you, the hope of Glory. "Let your speech be seasoned with grace" (Colossians 4:6), for doing so, you are revealing Christ in you.

10. Remember, if you are not enjoying Jesus, then no one will be in hurry to get to know Him.

11. Do not be surprised if you come under attack. Let other believers pray for you.

12. Do not bring your dog. It is considered a curse. It is said that when Mohammed was running from his enemy, a dog barked at him, and he cursed it. I have noticed that a lot of secular Muslims do not have an issue with dogs, and some even keep them as pets, but it is wise to use discernment.

13. Talk about what you have in common instead of your differences— like family, friends, neighbors, and what they value, fear of God. Remember: especially with Jews and Muslims, who trace their belief of one God through Abraham, it is always good to begin with what they know of God and of Christ! The objective is that they might come to know Him on a personal level. The Apostle Paul said in 1 Corinthians, "I have become all things to all people that I might by all means save some." Complimenting and encouraging someone is always acceptable and is considered kind in every culture.

14. Pray over your food. It is what we do. Pray audibly, if it is okay, but I have found silent prayer to be very powerful. You are asking a blessing and giving thanks for the occasion, but also it is a good time to ask your Jesus to give you some pointers.

15. Try not to challenge her beliefs, for she will challenge them herself after she has been exposed to the irresistible beauty and love of the Jesus in the Scriptures and the Jesus in your life. There should be no debate, no

quarrels—just offer her the Cross, where all the treasures she has ever longed for are hidden.

16. Do not change your normal routine or your Christian practices for fear of offending. If you are working under grace, I doubt that you will offend anyone. Often, when other faiths have an opportunity to see the love of Christ revealed in all its fullness through our lives and in the Scripture, they find life with Christ quite compelling. After all, grace does have an irresistible quality to it. God will reveal Himself to them when Jesus is revealed by the Spirit.

As I am writing this book, I have been receiving speaking engagements from my previous book, *From the Crescent to the Cross*. I am also involved with my previous assignments of volunteering, mentoring, and being part of a "prodigal" group.

Suddenly, out of nowhere, the Lord told me, with His matter-of-fact attitude, to stop volunteering and to stop my involvement with the prodigal group. Strangely enough, He never said anything about my mentoring. As a matter of fact, He gave me even more sisters to build up and strengthen. But He made it clear that my time with the prodigal group and my volunteer ministry with dementia patients were to be put on hold for now. I have been through this before, so I was not surprised, and I thought to myself, *Well, my Jesus has other plans*. So, no resisting required.

This was a profound reminder of what He is making of me and who I am becoming in Him. I never thought in my wildest dreams that I would be this person! He makes all things new. It is glorious! Looking back, it was not all of a sudden after all. Almost a year ago, God had given me Jeremiah 31:16-17:

Thus says the LORD: Refrain your voice from weeping, and your eyes from tears; For your work shall be rewarded, says the LORD, and they shall come back from the land of the enemy. There is hope in your future, says the LORD, That your children shall come back to their own border.

It was very clear. I do not know when, and it might well be after I transition to heaven, but the assurance of my prodigals coming home is sure with certainty—even though I would like to see them coming home to JESUS while alive in this world, perhaps so that I can have my bragging rights! But His will, not mine, be done. And yes, I have always prayed for my prodigals, every day, and I always will, and not only mine but all of my sisters'. I am continually reminded to be persistent, and I guess that "being persistent" meant to me that I had to be part of the prodigal group. That proved not to be the case at all. It meant that I have to be persistent in pursuing God, and when God gives me an assurance that a prayer has been or is being answered, then I should trust Him and move on with His plans.

Today I remind my Jesus of His promise for my prodigals and thank Him for His patience, mercy, and grace, and for the way He continues to bless them in every way, even though they do not give Him glory. But I do, because everything they have is from Him, and I am humbled by His goodness. Living in a broken world is a painful thing to endure, but as Christians, we are required to endure our prodigals whether they are our kids, our friends, our relatives, or the world. By God's grace, we love, pray, and wait patiently. This does not mean that we approve, but we give the opportunity and the room for God to display His Glory, and thus we endure our prodigals, the world, and each other.

Not being part of the prodigals group in person and not volunteering gave me a wonderful anticipation about what God was up to…

# chapter five

# God's Ways Are Not Our Ways

WHAT GOD had revealed was amazing. It started with His providing an opportunity for my Kenny and me to study the book of Romans. The fact that our beloved church, by chance, happened to be teaching on the book of Romans for both the women's and men's studies on Tuesday nights. By chance? No, by God's infinite wisdom!

So we began Romans together, which was really a blessing because we were able to discuss and study together what God was telling us in His Word. Romans has always been special for both of us. It is from this book that my husband and I learned how to get hold of the mystery of Grace regarding faith. This has been truly freeing for both of us! We never get tired of hearing about it over and over again. I am thankful for our church, which remains faithful to teach the Word of God.

So I settled into thinking, "I will continue to write this book and attend to speaking engagements and my mentoring." Just a short time later, God moved on me again, telling me that I needed to call a sister whom I have not talked to for four years. I began to look for her phone number. It did not exist any longer, but by the grace of God, her home number was still functioning. I left a brief message, which led to her calling me right away. We had sweet fellowship and wondered why we had stayed apart for so long. We laughed, we cried, and we shared all that God has done in our lives. My beautiful, precious sister has been diagnosed with Parkinson's disease, and I was moved with grief. But she comforted me, telling me that she had Parkinson's, but Parkinson's did not have her. I was in tears by this time, but they were tears of joy, and I was strengthened by her faith.

I brought her up to speed about all that God has been doing in my life, including the book that I had just written, and she jumped for joy. She asked if we could have lunch. I agreed. Little did I know that she had told so many sisters that I have collected through the years (including some new ones) about what has been happening with me, and they were delighted to hear all that God has done!

I also was amazed at how far each one of us had come. It solidified the fluidity of our faith as we realized how God increases and enlarges our hearts and continues to move us upward, making us streams of living water, which is forever moving and bending. It's not religion but the life of God.

I was surprised to learn how much we had progressed since the last time that we had seen each other! We are both calmer, gentler, and less dogmatic than we used to be, and we are learning to love God, to enjoy Him, and even learning to dance with Him! We thank Him, we praise Him. We just had not realized how much we had grown in His grace! And we had learned not to worry too much about working for God but to just enjoy Him, letting Him work through us. It was an eye-opening experience. We are enjoying our Jesus and each other as He opens the doors of opportunity that He wants us to go through.

I am so blessed to have a healthy relationship with my sisters, whether they are in the local church or other churches where God has sown His seeds of friendship and sisterhood. One God, one faith, one Lord—amazing!

As I am writing this book, the destruction that the radical Muslims cause is continuing around the world, domestically and internationally. I am discouraged and sheepish about writing this book, afraid that it will not be received well. America seems to be at a crossroads for her soul, for she is fighting to find the balance between safety and benevolence. It doesn't help when we have a government and media that are determined to divide us by race, gender, or religion. But I believe that America will find her way of reconciling Justice and Mercy. Christians view America and the world the way that God views them: with tender eyes, saying, "Come, let us reason together," for why should you die? So, we continue steadfastly, not backing away from any challenge, because we have God, who presides over us. So while the world is in a state of confusion, my sisters and I are on our bended knees, asking our Jesus for the souls of the lost for Him. We are hungry for them, reminding ourselves that this is not our home. This encourages me and reassures me that His people give up their lives everyday for others, because we have His DNA. That blesses me!

So we are enduring this crazy chaos, recognizing that we are the light that is shining in this dark, twisted world, so that our God can draw many daughters to Himself and chase away darkness.

The immigrant woman whom we are about to mentor and guide will experience God's forgiveness of sin through the Cross and will enjoy the new life with Him through the resurrected life given by the Holy Spirit, as she defeats death. There is *no fear of Death!* I feel immeasurable comfort knowing that I don't have to be afraid of death, because one cannot live until they learn how to die. And Christianity teaches us how to die so that we may live.

There is a flame of fire burning inside every immigrant woman—a flame of hope for a future that, for the first, time she feels may be within reach, that she may choose her destiny and be free to express herself. But it will take time to develop and to come into her own, and during her journey, there will be perilous times and danger of losing her "authenticity." So I believe that this is where the daughters of Abraham (Christian sisters) will be a great asset to her, guiding her to keep what is special and valuable in her culture but, at the same time, embracing the freedom, the opportunity, and the fluidity of Christianity in the American culture through mentoring. For our Jesus loves her much. Make no mistake: there are other forces fighting for her soul—Satan, the world, and the flesh, through feminism, the media, materialism, etc., all of which will feed her flesh and not her spirit.

Letting go of what she once believed about God will also take time, and it will be the work of the Holy Spirit, not us. So once again we should share the truth, and she should never have a doubt about what we believe, which is the truth in the face of Christ.

Not long ago, I had the privilege of speaking in an affluent Chinese church. It was for a women's luncheon during Thanksgiving time. Most of the attendees were students and well-to-do women who were scouting out how to "acquire" a piece of America. I was given thirty minutes with a translator to convince them that Christianity was the religion of choice.

Because of all this, it was important for me to find point of connection. It turned out that freedom would be that point, for I myself knew something about not having freedom of expression, just like them.

Here is my 15-minute speech:

"I am thankful to have freedom of speech.

"I am thankful to have freedom of Religion [and I lifted up my Bible] because I live in a country that allows me to choose my Religion without any fear. I found this Book that reveals the true and living God."

[Then I had to tap into what the Chinese culture values: wisdom, good fortune or blessing, knowledge and respect.]

I told them, "In this book you will learn about this amazing God, and as you get to know Him you will experience His infinite, irresistible love. The God who wrote this book promises Wisdom, how to help you make good decisions, how to get along with others. It promises peace and gives tranquility. It enriches your personal life and teaches you how to love others without any strings attached. It is a remedy for depression and worries. It is the answer Book for life's complicated questions. It clearly explains the origin of the universe. In this book you will find:

The first two chapters portray the absolute perfection of God when He created the world. Chapter three explains the fall of man and the chaos that ensued. This chaos continues all the way until it reaches the last two chapters of the Bible. Between the first two chapters and the last two lies the story of God's plan for this broken world: God promises a Redeemer, the Old Testament ends, and God is silent for four hundred years. Jesus is born into this world and is not received by most, but "as many as received Him, He promised them to be the children of God." Two thousand fifteen years later, some are still coming to Him and receiving the promise. And, sadly, some are refusing. God has given us the freedom to choose Him or to reject Him.

The last two chapters showcase the perfect world that is to come. The Bible begins with perfection and ends with perfection. Meanwhile, we are given the freedom to choose.

I concluded my talk by saying that even if you have no interest in knowing this amazing God, you should still read this Book just for its rich mastery of the English language. It will greatly improve your vocabulary. (I said this jokingly, but their interest was aroused.)

I finished by saying that this Book is a black-and-white portrait of a king who is inviting you to a beautiful banquet. In those few minutes, I encouraged them to think about God and the purpose of life. I heard later that one girl came to Jesus, and I prayed that the seed that was planted would flourish and produce fruit.

I enjoy visiting different churches, and as I do, the heart of my Jesus is clearly displayed in these believers, and I am encouraged and blessed to see how our God is moving in the hearts of His people toward the strangers among us. Our Lord cares about the widows and the fatherless (Deuteronomy 10:18; 14:29; 24:20; 26:13; Job 24:21, etc.). As I am given opportunities to speak in different churches, I am learning the different styles of worship and preaching and seeing how the Body of Christ celebrates their beloved Jesus, and it is glorious! My Jesus gives me the right message for each one of them, and they and I are both blessed.

As I speak to different congregations, I notice that most of my audience are among the silver-haired population. This observation puzzled me until I heard my beloved Jesus saying to me in my heart, "These are the ones who need assurance to not be afraid to do the works that I have for them, because they grew up times when America was divided and have been through wars, prejudice, and depression and were fearful of losing America as they know it." Every generation has its own challenges, and for them, they think that America belongs to white mature Americans and their offspring. But they are sweet and easily entreated when I explain to them that America belongs to all of us and that being a good steward is a responsibility for us all.

I thank them for giving us a beautiful country and ask them to pray for the generations after them. I also remind them that they are Christians and are required to be kind and hospitable toward strangers, having the heart of our Lord and Savior. I tell them not to fear, for we have our God watching over us. After I shared my own journey to the heart of God, one woman came up to me and said, "If the new immigrants are going to have a heart like yours, then we do not have to be afraid, do we?"

I was moved, and replied, "Pray that there will be many more." She said she would, and I was blessed, because when we do not share our hearts, we either are or become afraid of each other.

As seasoned Americans come to terms with this ever-shrinking world, I am encouraged by their immovable faith, which draws them to the heart of God and their willingness to listen to this sister of theirs. I am thankful for this group.

There is another group on the horizon that is stirring my spirit—the millennials. I think that I will dedicate a chapter to them, for they are very special and have a tender heart toward the young unbelievers.

# chapter six

# Telling Others about Jesus

AS WE BEGIN to reveal our Jesus to others, it is important to avoid telling them that He will always meet their material wants and needs, because that is not true. Even though He is certainly capable of giving us whatever He desires, that should never be our focus. It should be on Him and Him alone, and I have a hunch that the new immigrants have a better understanding in this matter than Americans because they are not as materially minded as we are.

In the Old Testament, our God promised a land and material blessings to the children of Israel. He did not do this for the church. He promises us a *spiritual* blessing, which is God Himself. He gave *Himself* to us, and that is far more excellent than, and superior to, anything in the world. The Bible tells us that we *will* have trials and trouble in this world. I was amazed as I read what people of faith went through in Hebrews 11:36-37 ("trials of mockings and scourgings, yes, and of chains and imprisonment. They were stoned, they were sawn in two, were tempted, were slain with the

sword...wandered about in sheepskins and goatskins, being desti-
tute, afflicted tormented..."). But look at what He has given to us: the
broken relationship is restored, and we are given a new life! The restoration comes through the Cross and the resurrection gives new life.

Just think about that for a moment, please. We have God, and
He is going to see us through. Oh, how amazing it is when we first
realize that God is for us, which means no fear, no worries; we have
been forgiven, restored, and healed spiritually to enjoy this amazing
fellowship with the living God. Glorious? Yes, but not only that! He
says that "Eye has not seen, nor ear heard, Nor have entered into the
heart of man the things which God has prepared for those who love
him" (2 Corinthians 2:9).

"So let us showcase this truth, which is much more excellent
than anything else." Oh yes, He will meet our needs but not our
wants, if He chooses to. Our

God is more interested in our spiritual growth and desires to do
life with us so we can participate with Him His plan for this broken
world. His desire is for us and our desire should for Him.

Teach the new believer to seek the Blesser instead of the blessing,
and she will be blessed. "Seek first the Kingdom of God..." (Matthew
6:33). They are forgiven; now teach them how to know the Forgiver.

Many of our children go astray because we fail to present God
as the person He is. And perhaps you have inadvertently told them
that God will hear their prayers and give them whatever they ask
without adding "according to His will." Yes, God always answers
our prayer: It may be "Yes," "No," or "Wait." So when He does not
come through for them according to their wish, they equate that with
the idea that God does not love them. We simply must be careful of
promising something our Lord did not promise.

What He *has* promised is far more gratifying than satisfying
one's instant desires. He promises the fruit of the Spirit: love, joy,
peace, longsuffering, kindness, goodness, faithfulness, gentleness,

self-control, and much more. Make no mistake: our God hears our prayers and answers them, but we must learn to be satisfied with the answer He gives. So it might be wise not to try to predict how God is going to engage them. Sometimes we get so desperate for people to believe in Him that we tell them how God is going to solve all their ills and misfortunes, and in some cases (as we should know from our own experiences), it gets worse before it gets better. We must simply share what God says about them in His Word. It is complete and beautiful just the way it is, and we do not need to add to it in order to make it more attractive. Let us expose the *whole counsel* of God, which is the Word of God in its totality. Knowing the character of God in His Word is very important when witnessing to unbelievers, including who God is and what He has done. That is why it is imperative to know the Word of God yourself.

I am always amazed at how many Christians who do not know the Word of God are still trying to witness to people, even though they themselves are not convinced that what they are saying is true because they do not have a good understanding of the Word of God. Regarding that, I am blessed to have a church that teaches the Word of God, verse by verse, from Genesis to Revelation. (And that reminds me: our church is studying the book of Revelation as I write this book… Glorious!)

It is good to be prepared to give an answer for the hope we have in Christ, which is hidden in His Word, and it is a treasure for which we have to dig. First Peter 3:15: "But sanctify the Lord God in your hearts, and always be ready to give a defense to every one who asks you a reason for the hope that is in you with meekness and fear." Knowing the Word of God not only prepares you to share it, but it also grounds you in knowing God Himself.

It is in my heart to give an overview of the Bible in the hope of creating a thirst and hunger in my sister's heart for two reasons: 1) To help the Christian sister receive at least a general knowledge of this amazing book, which is the Word of God. 2) To help the new believer to study the Bible by giving a short background of each book of the Bible and to foster an interest in this incredible Book of Life. I remember how hard it was for me to study the Word as someone who had never had a foundation in the Christian faith or the Bible. Becoming a Christian is simple. It begins with hearing and understanding who Jesus is and what He has done in order to have you. He went to the cross on your behalf to remove the enmity between you and a Holy God, so that you could be forgiven. Then He rose again from death to restore you to new life! The Cross is the picture of remission of sin, and the resurrection is to portray the new life where we enjoy God and He enjoys you.

The way to have this life of knowing your God and enjoying Him forever is hidden in His Word. That is why a Christian cannot enjoy and experience God without knowing His Word (the Bible). And even though we are not perfect, through the Word we are helped by the Holy Spirit, and it is through this that we grow and mature in the faith and become good witnesses (in other words, through the Word and the Spirit). In His Word He teaches us to "talk the talk and to walk the walk." This is how we learn to talk to God and to enjoy Him. He guides, He protects, He gives wisdom to handle the complex issues of life. "To know the Bible is to know God." No other faith gives us the ability to talk to God and have a close intimate relationship with Him.

This Bible overview is designed to help the seeker to have some understanding of each book of the Bible and to create a thirst and hunger for the Word of God, because it is truly the bread and the water of life.

The commentaries are gleaned from Dr. J. Vernon McGee. The translation is the New King James Version (NKJV). As you study the commentary, you also need to study each book in a careful manner, asking for direction with the help of the Holy Spirit. You will see what each book has meant in my own life along with the life verses that have meant so much to me. Studying the entire 66 books of the Bible has been a blessing and a great privilege, helping me to know my God better, and I am forever grateful for that opportunity. I will never be the same. You will notice throughout the next chapters that I will say often, "This is one of my favorite books!"

I have a hunch that the future church will become home churches, whether because of persecution or because of people growing bored and disappointed with the "big church" programs. People today are lonely, tired, and seeking to connect in genuine relationships with others and with God Himself in places where they can let their guard down and enjoy people with whom they have a connection, getting to know them, praying, worshiping, and studying the Word of God together, breaking bread and enjoying a meal together. In that case, the relationship with God and others is more complete, and the Cross comes into view. We should think of the picture of "vertical to God, horizontal to others," just as it was in the early church. I believe that we are coming full circle, which is really not a bad thing. It is simply going back to basics, which is likely where we need to be.

With that said, I want to continue with this: Mentoring and teaching the new believer in a home setting is of great benefit before we introduce them to the church on Sunday morning, because the pastor may be teaching on a subject that the new believer is not ready to digest yet.

One young lady with whom I was sharing the goodness of God decided to come to church with us. She had no background in Christianity, and the pastor happen to be teaching on God's view on homosexuality and how homosexuals will be judged. Needless to say, she stormed out of the building, traumatized, and vowed not come back to the church. Our pastor was simply teaching the Word of God, and I did not realize that he was teaching this particular passage of the Bible, or else I would have prepared her and reassured her to wait till to the end, because he always closes with the inexpressible Grace of God. But, sadly, she did not hear the good part. I found out later that she had some friends who are practicing this lifestyle, and she decided that she has no room for a God like this.

Such is the dilemma that faces the millennial generation—almost every one of them knows someone who is into this practice or who struggles with it. This is why we have to pray and ask our God to give us wisdom mingled with grace and *mercy* without compromising the *truth*. In the coming chapter, I will be looking closely at our Millennials and how we might gain some understanding about how to engage them.

It may seem that I am deviating from the subject of the immigrants, but I believe there is a connection, because our Millennials have the fortitude to connect with the new immigrants, since to them the world is one big mass without borders. Understanding their worldview will help us to build and nurture them so that they can be great disciples for our Jesus. And truly, isn't that what our Lord is all about—the World? He never told us to have borders but to go into all the world and preach the gospel. We are blessed to have a generation that is so tuned in to this call and who are global thinkers and trekkers.

I am praying that God will provide me an opportunity to be part of what our Lord is doing in this unique generation. The millennial believers have an advantage over the nonbelieving Millennials in that they tend to be connected with others, and there is an incredible bond, due to of their common faith, because of which they learn to listen to, share with, and pray together with others. This is huge and is also very attractive to nonbelievers who are then able to connect with the Christians because of their love for one another and for them!

# chapter seven

# Christian Millennials— The Chosen Generation

## *A Generation without Borders*

MILLENNIALS HAVE SURPASSED baby boomers as the nation's largest living generation, according to population estimates released by the government. They comprise the generation born between 1979-2001. Described as individualistic, they hate to be labeled as Millennials and can at times be narcissistic.

So just who are these Christian Millennials? This generation was born for "such a time as this" (Esther 4:14). No other generation has had the world at their fingertips (by means of technology), and with that comes an amazing opportunity for the "kingdom of light."

This so-called information highway did not appear by accident but by the perfect will of God. Just as He used the Roman Empire to build roads to connect the world so that the Gospel could reach the known world, so is He doing the same thing through technology in our world today. Glorious!

Whoever would have imagined thirty years ago that you could sell or buy a goat somewhere in the outer parts of the earth from the comfort of your home with a click of your smart phone? Or that a farmer in Ethiopia could sell his coffee beans in Seattle? Wonder of wonders! And our infinite God has put these Millennials right in the middle of this amazing period in our history, because history began and ends with our beloved Savior and Lord. History is indeed His story.

The unseen web of superhighways is evolving every day, and only our God knows where it ends. But I know that it will be for His Glory. With that said, let us take a look at this special generation: the millennial believers.

To begin with, they are worshipers of the true and living God. They are poets, composers, and singers, for and to our God, in Spirit and in truth. They are the artists. They paint the beauty of God's creation and the agony of pain in a world that is out of tune with God. They hear the cry of the human soul and they are action takers. They have no tolerance for bigotry or social injustice. They are tolerant and patient with the lost and have a great capacity to love. They are quick to extend the scepter of Grace to those who disagree with them, and they are less judgmental than many of their predecessors. They are tough on us parents, because they think that we are inflexible—and rightly so, at times. They are raw and transparent. They hate hypocrisy and are suspicious of politics and government.

But they love Jesus and the world for which He died. Their music is deep and touches the soul. They sing beautiful songs to our Savior, and He is personal to them. They are not afraid of the outside world. They are the travelers, backpackers, and couch surfers. They tend to be minimalist and have learned to live with little. They are approachable and easy to connect with as they are not easily offended or taken aback by different cultures. They tend to be globally minded and make great missionaries.

Because we live in a broken world, our beloved Millennials also have their flaws. Some of them, due to their youth, are impatient and may lack depth. Others are not as grounded in the Word as they should be, and as a result they are vulnerable to deception and may be easily misled by a pseudo-Christianity that promotes love without the Truth, which is not love at all. And since they are products of our education system, they tend to be squeamish about contending for the faith. Some of these have grown up in the church and in Christian homes and seemed to be easily fatigued about the issues of faith. But God is still at work, and they have soft hearts toward the downtrodden and marginalized. The ones who encounter Jesus at college are generally the ones who are fruitful at this time, because they already know something about the emptiness of this world.

I have had the honor of meeting and getting to know many of these Millennials at both Christian universities and secular colleges as well, and what I have seen has blessed me much and has encouraged me, knowing that our sweet Lord and Savior is with this unique generation in ways that you and I never imagined. When I realized this, I truly wept for joy. They are eager to know more about the new immigrants in our midst. Some have even moved to the areas where there is a colony of immigrants in order to be a light to them and to introduce them to the love of Christ as they represent Him. They are indeed ambassadors for our Lord.

I have also witnessed, in a state-owned university, a Christian student body that was openly worshiping and sharing their testimonies in the square of the university grounds. I was shocked to see Christians openly speaking about their Savior, because that is not what I hear in Christian circles. But our God is moving in the hearts of our beloved Millennials, and it is awesome to see. In colleges, I have seen students from all over the world. What an amazing opportunity our young believers have to share the gospel with these young foreigners who are going back to their country after they finish their education, prayerfully with Jesus in their heart. These foreign students are the future leaders of their countries. Our God is up to something wonderful! Christian intervarsity is alive and well in our secular colleges.

Someone shared with me about these young Christian students who are coming to the Lord and are having visions of being martyred for the faith. They are asking prayer for strength to be able to go through the persecution when it comes and that they will not deny their beloved Savior—not asking to be spared but to be able to die for the One who died for them. I tell you, I was quite undone when I heard this, but I was much strengthened by their unrelenting faith. I will be praying for them, and I ask others to pray as well.

A few things to keep in mind when engaging our Millennials: pray, be patient, employ active listening skills, ask open-ended questions, offer encouragement, guidance, and especially the foundational understanding of God's Word and the plan of Salvation. This is what is going to ground them in the faith. And because they live in a world of instant gratification, some tend to be impatient and easily discouraged when the expected results are delayed.

Mature Christian mentors are so valuable in their lives. We can guide them and encourage them to take a break from their gadgets and truly connect. I realize that they may think they are connecting, but you can only truly connect with people by knowing them personally and sharing your innermost thoughts and feelings (especially about our Savior). If you just put your thoughts out there and say what others want to hear, that is not a connection at all! And that is why our believing Millennials could be a great asset to a world that is lonely and starving for human connection. It is so important to invest in this young generation!

This is why both millennial believers and new immigrant believers grow strong roots when planted in home Bible study groups, where they are fed and nurtured by mature believers who are filled with the Spirit and who protect them from false teachings and burdensome "keeping of the law." Here they learn that it is not by works, nor by rules and rituals—but by Grace, through faith, that one may connect with our Savior and enjoy Him as He enjoys each of us.

In this environment, each group will learn the Word of God, learn to worship their God, and will break bread together so that they can get to know their God and each other. And as they join the local church and mature in the faith through discipleship, then they are already being equipped to disciple others as they themselves have been discipled. Oh! How glorious that day will be, when we own and nurture our beloved Millennials so that they can bring the world under the instruction of our Lord and Savior! And when the new immigrants are finally able to put all their shame and marginalized lives down and walk away with Jesus—free, with their hands lifted up and their hearts united, as one millennial singer sang.

# SECTION TWO

## Overview of the Bible: The Book of Books

*Born in the East and clothed in Oriental form and imagery, the Bible walks the ways of all the world with familiar feet, and enters land after land to find its own [people] everywhere. It has learned to speak in hundreds of languages to the heart of man. It comes into the palace to tell the monarch that he is the servant of the Most High, and into the cottage to assure the peasant that he is a son of God. Children listen to the stories with wonder and delight, and wise men ponder them as parables of life. It has a word of peace for the time of peril, a word of comfort for the time of calamity, a word of light for the hour of darkness. Its oracles are repeated in the assembly of people, and its counsels whispered in the ear of the lonely. The wicked and the proud tremble at its warnings, but to the wounded and the penitent, it has a mother's voice. The wilderness and the solitary place have been made glad by it, and the fire on the hearth has lit the reading of its well-worn pages. It has woven itself into our dearest dreams; so that love, friendship, sympathy, and devotion, memory, and hope put on the beautiful garments of its treasured speech, breathing of frankincense and myrrh.* —HENRY VAN DYKE

This overview of the Bible is gleaned from *Guidelines for the Understanding of the Scriptures* by Dr. J. Vernon McGee on *Through the Bible Radio Network*. (Translation is New King James Version.)

# chapter eight

# The Pentateuch (Five Books of Moses)

*These five books of the Bible were given primarily to the Jewish people and contain many truths and blessings for others, including ourselves, as our Lord Jesus is revealed and the blueprint of life is given regarding God and His concern for humanity. The law is given, God's love is shown, and the inability of man to keep the law is clearly demonstrated.*

## 1. THE BOOK OF GENESIS

**Author:** *Believed to be Moses*

**Theme:** *The book of beginnings, or births*

Genesis falls into two natural divisions:

1. The book of the birth of Heaven and the Earth (Genesis 2:4)

2. The book of the birth of men (Genesis 5:1)

**Key:** *The generations of mankind—how it all began*

**Summary:**

This book beautifully narrates the beginning of the earth and the creation of humanity. It clearly states the absolute perfection of God's creativity and the fall of humanity. Our first parents, Adam and Eve, dwelt in perfect fellowship and life with God; chaos began and remains until Revelation 21. Yet through all of this, the roots of grace were being sown. God's perfect plan to redeem the souls of men continues, beginning in Genesis 3:15, where the *Gospel* is first preached. Genesis 3 explains what went wrong, and God counteracts this with His beautiful plan of redemption.

The book of Genesis is a bittersweet book, portraying mankind's colossal failure and his wicked heart, along with God's amazing grace and His desire to restore man. The book of Genesis reveals a detailed timeline of the origin of the earth and humanity, and if you can come to terms with this book, you won't have any trouble believing in God and His plan for you! The rest of the Bible will come alive in your mind and heart because you will have understood its very foundation. To sum up, the book of Genesis contains the early record of humanity and so is extremely important to our understanding of God and His plan for mankind.

## 2. THE BOOK OF EXODUS

**Author:** *Moses*

**Theme:** *"Exodus" means "the way out"*

We learn that Redemption is by blood and by power. This message is also stated in Hebrews 11:23-29, in which the faith of Moses and his obedience to God is described beautifully.

**Key Verse:** *Exodus 20:2*

"I am the LORD your God, who brought you out of the land of Egypt, out of the house of bondage."

**Summary:**

Seventy souls of Jacob entered Egypt, and nearly 2+ million left Egypt. Moses was the leader, and his life is divided into three 40-year periods:

- 40 years in Pharaoh's palace in Egypt
- 40 years in the desert with the Midianites
- 40 years in the wilderness as the leader of Israel

God must take Moses out of Egypt so that He can take Egypt out of Moses. He leads him out into the desert, where Moses makes a living as a shepherd. God reveals Himself to Moses in a burning bush and sends him back to Egypt to deliver God's people, the Israelites.

Instead of allowing the people to go with Moses, the Bible says that Pharaoh's heart is "hardened," which means that God caused Pharaoh to reveal his wicked heart. God's judgment was poured out on Egypt, and seven plagues were released, which represented the seven gods the Egyptians worshiped.

**Important Events:**

- The Passover was instituted
- The Israelites left Egypt
- The Red Sea was divided
- The Ten Commandments were given
- The Law was given and the people agreed to obey it (Exodus 24:1-3)
- The blueprint for the Tabernacle was given, and the temporary version of it was constructed
- The glory of the Lord filled the Tabernacle

The Book of Exodus begins in gloom and ends in Glory! At the end of the book, the people are at Mount Sinai. My favorite verse is Exodus 15:11, "Who is like You, O Lord, among the gods? Who is like You, glorious in holiness, Fearful in praises, doing wonders?" (NKJV)

## 3. THE BOOK OF LEVITICUS

**Author:** *Moses*

**Theme:** *Marking Time*

At this point in time, the children of Israel are marking time at Mount Sinai. The book opens and concludes at the same geographical spot. Leviticus gives the order of worship in the tabernacle. God moves into the tabernacle and speaks from there rather than from Mount Sinai.

**Key Concept:** *The Holiness of God*

**Summary:**

This book was given to Israel for direction in how to live as a holy nation in fellowship with a holy God. It was a code of law for the total well-being of Israel (physical, moral, and spiritual). Leviticus is a book that describes God's desire and requirements regarding worship, sacrifice, ceremony, ritual, liturgy, instructions, washings, etc. It utilizes physical exercises to teach spiritual truths. And it is the prelude to what Christ has accomplished for us so that today we may come to the throne of God through the Cross.

**Message:**

Leviticus teaches that the way to God is through sacrificial " atonement," which means that sin is "covered." Animal sacrifice merely *covered up* sin, but it did not *take away* sin. Only the blood of Christ takes away our sin. Leviticus teaches that our walk with God is by sanctification. We are to be "holy," which means to be set apart for a special purpose.

**To Review:**

- Genesis: Man is ruined
- Exodus: Man is redeemed
- Leviticus: Man is worshiping

| EXODUS | LEVITICUS |
|---|---|
| Exodus offers pardon | Leviticus offers purity |
| God's approach to man | Man's approach to God |
| Christ is Savior | Christ is Sanctifier |
| Man's guilt is prominent | Man's defilement is prominent |
| God speaks out of Mount Sinai | God speaks in the tabernacle |
| Man is made right to God | Man is kept right to God |

(Chart from *Thru the Bible Commentary* by J. Vernon McGee)

## 4. THE BOOK OF NUMBERS

**Author:** *Moses*

**Theme:**

A sort of *Pilgrim's Progress*—walking, wandering, working, warring, witnessing, and worshiping. It is the road map for the wilderness of the world.

**Key Passage:** *Numbers 14:29-31*

"The carcasses of you who have complained against Me shall fall in this wilderness, all of you who were numbered, according to your entire number, from twenty years old and above. Except for Caleb the son of Jephunneh and Joshua the son of Nun, you shall by no means enter the land which I swore I would make you dwell in. But your little ones, whom you said would be victims, I will bring in, and they shall know the land which you have despised."

**Summary:**

The attitude of unbelief has crystallized into actual disobedience. The light is focused on faith—and the Israelites failed. We see that they could not enter the Promised Land because of unbelief (Hebrews 3:19): and we learn to understand the peril of not progressing. A forty-day journey turned into forty years of wandering. Because of their unbelief, everyone twenty years and older died in the wilderness except for Joshua and Caleb, who believed in God's presence and His promises.

Numbers is a book that tells of a sad journey that has a happy ending. God moves forward with His plans because of His own faithfulness. People, on the other hand, moved backwards because of their unbelief.

## 5. THE BOOK OF DEUTERONOMY

**Author:** *Moses*

**Theme:** *The book of experience and obedience*

**Key:** *"Love and obey"*

- The coming of Christ (18:15-18)
- Love of God (4:37, 7:7-8, 23:5)
- Obedience to God (4:40, 11:26-28, 30:8-20)
- Love for God (6:4-5, 30:6, 30:16, 30:20)

Jesus quoted exclusively from this book when beating back Satan's temptation (Matthew 4:4-10, Luke 4:4-12).

**Summary:**

Moses spoke with God face to face. He knew God personally, and God "made known His ways known to Moses, His acts to the children of Israel" (Psalm 103:7). The children of Israel saw the acts of God, and yet they did not know Him. Moses knew His ways. The Book of Deuteronomy is the result of this intimate knowledge plus his experience of 40 years in the wilderness. Deuteronomy means "The Second Law" and is a commentary on the Mosaic Law.

A new generation is about to enter the land, none of whom were alive when the law was given, and it is interpreted after 38 years of experience in the wilderness, as new situations and problems arose that were not covered by the law. There needed to be an application of the law to real-life situations (example: Numbers 27:1-9: women's rights were given by our God). Giving the Israelites the land was *unconditional*; their prospering in the land was *conditional*. The condition was obedience. The law of blessing and cursing is narrated in this book. The people chose God, and God chose His people (Deuteronomy 26:16-19).

# chapter nine

# Historical Books of the Bible

*The historical books of the Bible include Joshua, Judges, Ruth, 1, 2 Samuel, 1, 2 Kings, 1, 2 Chronicles, Ezra, Nehemiah and Esther.*

## THE BOOK OF JOSHUA

**Author:** *Joshua*

Joshua's name means "Jehovah Is Salvation." This is the same as the name JESUS in the New Testament. Joshua was a great general, who had been born as a slave in Egypt and was 40 years old at the time of the Exodus. He was one of the spies in Numbers 14:30. Joshua was 80 years old when he received his commission from God. Joshua died at age 110.

**Theme:** *To complete redemption of the Jews from Egypt*

Salvation is not only redemption from hell but also redemption into heaven and fellowship with the living God.

Up to this point, Jehovah God had spoken by dreams, visions, or angelic ministries, and sometimes face to face, as in the case of Moses. During this next period, a new method of communication is introduced. The Law of Moses represents the written voice of God, to which they must pay very close attention (Joshua 1:8).

**Key verse:** *Joshua 1:3*

"Every place that the sole of your foot will tread upon I have given you, as I said to Moses."

Israel is promised earthly blessings, and the church is promised spiritual blessings (see Ephesians 1:3). Conflict and conquest accompany possessions, both to Israel and the church.

**Key word:** *"Possession"*

Israel's *ownership* of the land was unconditional (Genesis 15:7); but Israel's *possession* of the land was conditional (Deuteronomy 30:20). God gets the victory, and Israel gets deliverance and possession of the land. In Joshua, the land is entered, the land is divided, and Israel promised to obey God. A nation is born; promises are fulfilled (Joshua 21:43-45).

**Message:** *The faithfulness of God*

Rahab is remembered, the walls of Jericho were crumbled. Israel served the Lord all the days of Joshua, and all the days of the elders who outlived Joshua and had known the works of the Lord that He had done for Israel. Glorious!

## THE BOOK OF JUDGES

**Author:** *Unknown; perhaps Samuel*

After Joshua and all of his generation passed away, another generation arose after them who did not know God or the works that He had done for Israel.

**Theme:**

Backsliding and the amazing grace of God in recovering and restoring ruined lives. "Righteousness exalts a nation, but sin is a reproach to any people." (Proverbs 14:34)

**Key verse:** *Judges 21:25*

> *In those days there was no king in Israel; everyone did what was right in his own eyes.*

This is the last verse of the Book of Judges, which to me is the saddest time in Israel's history. It is the beginning of the end. Israel will demand to have a king instead of God, who was willing to be their King. We will see this as the Bible unfolds before our eyes.

**Purpose:**

The Book of Judges has a twofold purpose: Historically, it records the history of the nation, from the death of Joshua to Samuel, the last of the judges and the first of the prophets. It bridges the gap between Joshua and the rise of the monarchy. There was no leader to take Joshua's place in the way he had taken Moses' place. This was indeed the trial period of the Theocracy after they entered the land.

Morally, it was a time of deep declension of the people as they turned from their unseen leader (God) and descended, as the Scriptures describe, to the low level of "In those days there was no king in Israel, and every man did that which was right in his own eyes" (Judges 17:6, 21:25). Compare Judges 1:1 with Judges 20:18. This should have been an era of glowing progress, but instead it was a dark day of repeated failures.

The law they had promised to obey was fading in their everyday lives and hearts. Their high hopes and exuberant expectations failed because of their disobedience, and that resulted in disappointment. The nation fell into seven different apostasies, and God faithfully raised up judges to deliver them within a local and restricted area. Among those were Deborah, Barak, Jephthah, Gideon, Samson, and Samuel, the last Judge. This confused period resulted in three stages of decline:

1.  Religious apostasy (See especially chapters 17 and 18)

2.  Moral decadence (Everywhere, including the home, see chapter 19)

3.  Political anarchy (The state, see chapters 20, 21)

God's wonderful heart of mercy and grace is displayed even in this very sad book.

## THE BOOK OF RUTH

**Author:** *Possibly Samuel*

**Key verse:** *Ruth 3:18*

Then she said, "Sit still, my daughter, until you know how the matter will turn out; for the man will not rest until he has concluded the matter this day."

**Theme:** *The Kinsman Redeemer*

"A Bright Spot in the Dark Picture in the Time of the Judges"

**Features:**

- A love story in every sense of the word, yet without actually using the word "love."
- The story of a prodigal family who went to a far country.
- The law of kinsman redeemer is fully described here.

This book links the tribe of Judah with King David, which links to the genealogy of the Lord Jesus in the book of Matthew. The genealogy of the book is its most important documentation (Ruth 4:18-22). It is story of tenderness, sweetness, and loveliness. It begins with disobedience and ends with Redemption. My Jesus is all over this little book. In a sense, I am Ruth, redeemed by my lovely Savior—a Gentile redeemed by an Israelite. Glorious! Naomi portrays Israel. Ruth is viewed as the church, and Boaz is seen as a picture of Christ.

Ruth is a Gentile peasant woman who marries a Jewish prince. It is like our Jesus opening His arms to the Gentiles. We Gentiles are married to a Jewish Prince (Jesus)!

**Outline:**

Chapter 1: Ruth is the subject in the land of Moab

Chapter 2: Ruth is working in the field of Boaz

Chapter 3: She is in the threshing floor of Boaz

Chapter 4: She is in the heart and home of Boaz

## 1ST AND 2ND SAMUEL

**Authors:** *Samuel, Nathan, and possibly Gad*

The books of 1st and 2nd Samuel give us the origin of the kingdom. The authors may be Samuel, Nathan, and it is possible that even Gad may have contributed (but not certain).

**Themes:** *Prayer & The Kingdom*

- First Samuel opens with prayer, chapter 1:8-12.
- Second Samuel closes with prayer, chapter 24: 10-25.
- The Kingdom

**Summary:**

Israel moves from being a people governed by God [a Theocracy] to a people ruled by a human king, as noted in Hosea 13:11, "I gave you a king in My anger and took him away in My wrath."

The people choose King Saul to reign over them. Israel anoints their first human king, rejecting God as ruler over them (1 Samuel 8:7). Saul fails as king because he was disobedient to God.

God rejects Saul (1 Samuel 15:22-23). God chooses His own king and makes His covenant with David to rule over His Israel (1 Samuel 16:1-13). Pay special attention to 1 Samuel 16:7!

**Special Features:**

- The priest presents the people to God, and the prophet presents God to the people.
- Bad king: Saul was chosen by the people.
- Good king: David was chosen by God.

Samuel is the last Judge and the first prophet of Israel. The author of 1st and 2nd Samuel narrates the story of the kingdom with two kings who ruled. There were no longer judges ruling over them. It was now the king who ruled over the people. In these two books, prophets are instituted to represent God and to advise the king on how to rule the people according to God's requirements.

First Samuel ends with the death of Saul and his sons. Second Samuel continues with the message of 1st Samuel. It is given over entirely to the reign of King David. The life and times of David are very important because he is an ancestor of the true King [Jesus]. Second Samuel ends with David's sin of numbering the people, God's judgment against him, and His subsequent mercy toward King David (2 Samuel 24:10-25).

## 1ST AND 2ND KINGS

**Theme:**

The prominence of the prophet and the insignificance of the priest are shown in these two books. The books of 1st and 2nd Kings narrate:

- the death of king David
- the rise of King Solomon
- the building of the glorious Temple
- Israel becomes a beacon to the world, and all the king-doms of the earth sought King Solomon's wisdom, and Israel enjoyed a period of peace and prosperity. The books close with the division and collapse of the kingdom.

**Key Verses:** *2 Kings 17:22 and 25:21*

**Purpose:**

The throne on earth has failed to be in tune with the Throne in Heaven. In these books, the history of the nation is traced from the time of its greatest extent, influence, and prosperity under King David and Solomon to the division and, finally, the captivity and exile of both kingdoms.

## 1ST AND 2ND CHRONICLES

### *The Acts of the Old Testament*

**Author:** *Possibly Ezra*

Although the books of Kings and Chronicles cover the same history from King Saul through King Zedekiah, they are not duplications. In these two books, God goes over territory that has already been covered in order to add details and to emphasize certain ideas that He considers especially important. Of all the six books of 1st and 2nd Samuel, 1st and 2nd Kings, and 1st and 2nd Chronicles, my favorites are 1 and 2 Chronicles, because in these I see the tender heart of God. The Chronicles do not record the sin of David (when God forgives, He also forgets). In 1st Chronicles, *David* is the subject. In 2nd Chronicles, the *house of David* is prominent. Chronicles gives the history of Judea while practically ignoring the Northern kingdom (you will see why after reading 2nd Kings).

**Special Points:**

- The Temple and Jerusalem are featured prominently
- In Kings, the history of the nation is given from the perspective of the kings
- In Chronicles, the history of the nation is given from the perspective of the priests
- In Kings, the palace is central
- In Chronicles, the temple is central
- In Kings, the political history of the nation is recorded
- In Chronicles, the religious history is recorded
- In Kings, man's viewpoint is given
- In Chronicles, God's viewpoint is given

**Outline of 1st Chronicles:**

1.  Chapters 1-9: Genealogy

2.  Chapter 10: Saul's Reign

3.  Chapter 11-29: David's Reign

**Outline of 2nd Chronicles:**

1.  Chapters 1-9: Solomon's reign and the building of the Temple

2.  Chapters 10-36: Division of the kingdom and the history of Judah

**Key Verse:** *2 Chronicles 16:9*

"For the eyes of the LORD run to and fro throughout the whole earth, to show Himself strong on behalf of those whose heart is loyal to Him. In this you have done foolishly; therefore from now on you shall have wars."

# POST-CAPTIVITY BOOKS

*The post-captivity books record the return and restoration at Jerusalem after the years of Babylonian captivity as predicted by the prophet Jeremiah. Six books belong to this series, and they are divided into two groups:*

1.  Historical: Ezra, Nehemiah, Esther

2.  Prophetic: Haggai, Zachariah, Malachi (see Chapter 11)

## THE BOOK OF EZRA

**Author:** *Ezra*

Ezra is the "uniter." He began the first revival after the captivity by reading the Word of God.

**Theme:** *The Word of the Lord*

Ezra was the first to start a revival of studying the Bible. The importance of the Word of God in every aspect of the lives of His people—religious, social, business, and political—is shown.

**Key Verse:** *Ezra 9:4,10:3*

The people were troubled by the Word of the God of Israel and trembled, resulting in their making a covenant with the Lord to be obedient to His commandments.

After King Cyrus of Persia gave permission for the people of Judea to return to Jerusalem and rebuild the Temple, only 50,000 returned. Most of these were Levitical priests and Levites of the humbler and poorer class of people, who were rich in God's eyes.

## THE BOOK OF NEHEMIAH

**Author:** *Possibly Ezra*

**Theme:** *Building the wall of the city*

The emphasis in the book of Nehemiah is on building the wall of the city. (The emphasis in Ezra was building the temple.)

The majority of the Jewish people didn't return because they had prospered during their years of captivity. Chronologically, this is the last of the historical books. The Old Testament goes no further, as far as time is concerned. Nehemiah was a layman and cup bearer for

King Artaxerxes of Persia. Nehemiah hears bad news from Jerusalem that the people were in great distress, and the walls of the city were in ruins. Nehemiah weeps and prays, with fasting. **Nehemiah 1:4-11** is the heart of the book. Nehemiah and the people go to work to rebuild the wall and the gates.

When that is finished, the Word of God is read, and reform and revival take place. Sadly, the restoration was incomplete. The Jewish people were still not free from this time on up to the time of the Roman Empire. The New Testament opens with them under the rule of Rome. Nehemiah is a man of action and few words who has a close relationship with God.

**Key Word:** *"So"*

**Key Verses:** *Nehemiah 1:4 and 6:3*

"So it was, when I heard these words, that I sat down and wept, and mourned for many days; I was fasting and praying before the God of heaven." (1:4)

"So I sent messengers to them, saying, "I am doing a great work, so that I cannot come down. Why should the work cease while I leave it and go down to you? (6:3)

## THE BOOK OF ESTHER

**Author:** *Unknown (possibly Mordecai—see Esther 9:29)*

**Theme:**

Esther is the last of the historical books of the Bible and is one of only two books in the Old Testament named for a woman: Ruth is the story of a Gentile who married a Hebrew, while Esther is the story of a Hebrew woman who married a Gentile.

**Key Verse:** *Esther 4:14*

The name of God is not mentioned in the book; no divine title or pronoun refers to Him. The heathen king's name is mentioned 192 times. It is also true that God's name is not mentioned in the Song of Solomon, but every pronoun (with the exception of 8:6) refers to Him. Esther is a record of Israel, a nation that is on a self-chosen pathway. Opportunity had been given for the Jews to return under King Cyrus, but only a very small remnant had taken advantage of that opportunity. The books of Ezra and Nehemiah tell the story of those who did return. The book of Esther tells the story of those who did not return, but who chose, instead, the prosperity and luxury of Persia. They are out of the will of God, but they are not beyond His care. Deuteronomy 31:18 explains the reason that God's name does not appear in the book of Esther: *His face is hidden.* There is no mention of prayer or dependence upon God in this book.

**Message:** *The providence of God*

The book of Esther reveals the providence of God. Theologically, providence is the direction God gives to everything, animate and inanimate, good or evil. Practically, providence is the hand of God in the glove of history, and the glove will never move until He moves. God is at the steering wheel of the universe.

Providence means God is behind the scenes, shifting and directing them. Providence is the way God coaches the man on second base; it is the way God leads the man who will not be led. God remains in the shadows, keeping watch over His own. Anti-Semitism is clearly recorded in this book. (See Genesis 12:3). God comes through for His people. It is comforting to know.

# chapter ten

# Bible Books of Poetry & Wisdom

*The poetic books of the Bible include Job, Psalms, Proverbs, Ecclesiastes, and the Song of Solomon.*

## THE BOOK OF JOB

**Author:** *Unknown—possibly Elihu (Job 32: 6-17)*

**Date of writing:** *Unknown—perhaps during the patriarchal period*

**Theme:**

Job is the first of six poetic books in the Bible. You may notice that it is not rhythmic. Hebrew poetry is created by repeating an idea, which is called parallellism.

**Purpose:**

1. To reveal Job to himself.

2. To demonstrate that even the most upright man needs a Savior and he still needs to repent: "I have heard of You by the hearing of the ear, But now my eye sees You. Therefore I abhor myself, and repent in dust and ashes" (Job 42:5-6).

**Key verse:** *Job 1:21*

"Naked I came from my mother's womb, and naked shall I return there. The LORD gave, and the LORD has taken away; Blessed be the name of the LORD.

**Outline:**

1. Chapter 1:1-5: Job's prosperity and serenity

2. Chapter 1:6-12: Satan's slander of God and Job

3. Chapter 1:13-22: Job's loss of children and wealth

4. Chapter 2:1-6: God and Satan converse again

5. Chapter 2:7-10: Job's loss of health and wife's sympathy

6. Chapter 2:11–42:6: Dialogue as poetry with Job's friends, Eliphaz the Temanite, Bildad the Shuhite, Zophar the Naamathite, and Elihu the son of Barachel the Buzite

7. Chapter 38:1–42:6: Jehovah vs. Job. Even righteous Job failed to meet God's standard of Holiness. The book ends with Job's repentance. It is marvelous to see God's faithfulness

## THE BOOK OF PSALMS

*The Book of Psalms, the Book of Praise (the Hymn Book of the Temple)*

**Authors:** *Multiple*

King David, the "sweet psalmist of Israel," has 73 psalms attributed to him. Some "orphanic" (non-attributed) psalms could also have been written by David. And the others?

- Moses – 1 (Psalm 90)
- Solomon – 2
- The Sons of Korah – 11
- Asaph – 12
- Heman – 1 (Psalm 88)
- Ethan – 1 (Psalm 89)
- Hezekiah – 10
- Orphanic Psalms – 39

**Theme:** *Christ the Messiah is prominent (Luke 24:44)*

**Keyword:** *Hallelujah!*

**Key Psalm:** *Psalm 150*

The word "hallelujah" occurs 13 times in 6 verses (in the language of Heaven).

**Features:**

The psalms record deep devotion, intense feeling, exalted emotions, and dark dejection. Psalms play upon the keyboard of the human soul. This is the human heart attempting to unite with God's heart. This book has been called the epitome and anatomy of the soul and the garden of the Scriptures.

Although the Psalms have a peculiar Jewish application, they also express the deep feelings and longings of believing hearts in all generations. The Psalms are full of Christ. There is a more complete picture of Him in the Psalms than in the Gospel. For example:

- The gospel tells us that He went to the mountain to pray. Psalms gives us His prayers.

- The Gospels tells us that He was crucified. Psalms tells us what went on in His own heart during the crucifixion.

- The Gospels tell us that He went back to Heaven. The Psalms begin where the Gospels left off, and they show us Christ seated in Heaven.

Although all of the psalms have Christ as the object of worship, some are technically called "The Messianic Psalms." These record the birth, life, death, resurrection, glory, Priesthood, Kingship, and return of Christ. There are also imprecatory psalms, which can stumble the new believer because they contain prayers for judgment. These psalms came from a time of war, from people who were under the law and looking for justice and peace on the earth. On the contrary, the Christian is told to love and pray for one's enemies (Luke 6:27-36). This verse is a good guideline for the believer today.

Brief outline of the Pentateuch of Moses (The first five books of the Bible):

1. Genesis relates to Psalms 1-41: Blessedness, the Fall of Man, Recovery—**Mankind is in view**

2. Exodus relates to Psalms 42-72: Ruin and Redemption of Man—**Israel is in view**

3. Leviticus relates to Psalms 73-89: Darkness and Dawn —**The Sanctuary is in view**

4. Numbers relates to Psalms 90-106: Peril and Protection —**The Earth is in view**

5. Deuteronomy relates to Psalms 107-150: Perfection and Praise of the Word of God—**Heaven is in view**

Psalm 119 is an acrostic in the heart of Deuteronomy. It refers to the Word of God in almost every verse. It is the longest chapter in the Bible.

## THE BOOK OF PROVERBS

**Author**: *Solomon*

**Theme:** *This is a book of wisdom*

Proverbs contain short sentences describing what has been drawn from long experience. Although the book of Proverbs seems to be a collection of sayings without any particular regard for orderly arrangement, actually the contrary is true. The book tells us the story of a young man starting out in life.

His first lesson is given in Proverbs 1:7. Two "schools" bid to him and both send out their literature:

1. School of Wisdom.

2. School of fools

In chapter 8, he chooses the Academy of Wisdom, where he is taught how to acquire wisdom. In chapters 10-24, we are privileged to "sit in" with the young man in the classroom of Wisdom. In the Bible, wisdom is one of the attributes of God.

**Outline:**

1. Wisdom & folly are contrasted, chapters 1-9

2. The Proverbs of Solomon are ordered by Solomon, chapters 10-24

3. The Proverbs of Solomon are ordered by "the men of Hezekiah," chapters 25-29

4. The Oracle of Agur, an unknown sage, chapter 30

5. The Proverb of a mother to her son, Lemuel (who is believed to be Solomon himself), chapter 31

**My favorite passage:** *Proverbs 3:5-6*

---

*Trust in the LORD with all your heart, And lean not on your own understanding; In all your ways acknowledge Him, And He shall direct your paths.*

---

## THE BOOK OF ECCLESIATES

**Author:** *Solomon*

This book is the dramatic autobiography of Solomon's life when he "got away" from God. The word "Ecclesiastes" means Preacher or philosopher. This section of the Bible describes a person who is attempting to find contentment or happiness apart from God, and the narration reveals the absurdity of trying.

Solomon, who was the wisest of men, experienced every field of endeavor and pleasure known to man. His sad conclusion is that "All is Vanity." The word "vanity" means empty or worthless.

In Ecclesiastes we learn that without God we cannot be satisfied, even if we possess the whole world. (The heart is too large for the object, i.e, it is never content.) In the Song of Solomon we learn that if we turn away from the world and set our affections on Christ, we will not even be able to fathom the infinite preciousness of His Love. (The object is too large for the heart!)

God revealed to Job, who was a righteous man, that even Job was a sinner in God's sight. In Ecclesiastes, God shows the wisest man, Solomon, that he is a fool in God's sight.

**Key words:**

*"Vanity"* (occurs 37 times)

*"Under the sun"* (occurs 29 times)

**Outline:**

1. The problem is stated (chapter 1:1-3)—"All is vanity"

2. The experiment begins (chapters 1:4-12:12)—Seeking satisfaction in science, in wisdom, in pleasure, in materialism (living for the present), fatalism, egotism, religion, wealth, and morality

3. The result of the experiment (chapter 12:13-14)— Everything under the sun (the world) is vanity.

A right relationship with God at any age brings the only abiding satisfaction. What a difference between the man who lives "under the sun" and the man who is in Christ, and is seated in the Heavenlies with Him, far above all suns!

**Key verse:** *Ecclesiastes 12:14*

*For God will bring every work into judgment, Including every secret thing, Whether good or evil.*

## THE SONG OF SOLOMON

**Author:** *Solomon (chapter 1:1)*

Solomon wrote 1,005 songs (1 Kings 4:32), but we only have the Song of Songs. As the name would indicate, it is the best.

**Keywords:** *"Beloved" and "Love"*

"Beloved" (her name for him) and "Love" (his name for her)

**Key verses:** *6:3 and 8:7*

---

*I am my beloved's, And my beloved is mine. He feeds his flock among the lilies.*

---

---

*Many waters cannot quench love, Nor can the floods drown it. If a man would give for love all the wealth of his house, It would be utterly despised.*

---

**Meaning:**

The Song of Solomon is parabolic poem (i.e., expressed as a parable). It is the *interpretation*, not the *inspiration*, that causes the difficulty.

1. It depicts the glory of wedded love, a satisfied husband, and a devoted wife.

2. It displays God's love for Israel. The prophets frequently spoke of Israel as the wife of Jehovah. These two interpretations have been set forth by the scribes and rabbis of Israel and are accepted by the church. However, there are two other interpretations that can be gleaned from this.

The book also gives us a picture of Christ and the church. The church as the bride of Christ is a familiar figure in the Scriptures: 2 Corinthians 11:2, Ephesians 5:27, and Revelation 21. It portrays the communion of Christ with the individual believer. The soul's communion with Christ is clearly set forth and is the best interpretation. In my heart, this book speaks to me about the love of Christ for me and my love for Him.

**Story outline:**

The setting of the drama is the palace in Jerusalem. The key to the story is chapter 8:11. The story tells of the poor family of Ephraim, in which there is a girl who is similar to "Cinderella." The poverty of the family forces her to work in the vineyards, where she meets the young shepherd. The story of their love is described.

The young man leaves her with the promise that he will return. He is absent for a long time, and she begins to despair of his return when suddenly a word is shouted along the way that King Solomon is coming by! She is not interested and takes no further notice until word is brought to her that king Solomon wants to see her. She is puzzled until she is brought into his presence, where she recognizes him as her shepherd lover.

The underlying story of this beautiful book is about Jesus Christ and His love for the church, for the individual believer, and for Israel as well.

# chapter eleven

# Prophetic Books of the Bible

*The prophetic books of the Bible include five "major prophets" —Isaiah, Jeremiah, Lamentations, Ezekiel, Daniel—and twelve "minor prophets": Hosea, Joel, Amos, Obadiah, Jonah, Micah, Nahum, Habakkuk, Zephaniah, Haggai, Zachariah, and Malachi. (For background information please read 1 Peter 1:10-11 and 2 Peter 1:19-21.)*

THE PROPHETIC BOOKS are arranged into two categories: the major prophets and the minor prophets. This does not mean that one is more important than the other but may perhaps relate to the length of the book. It seems that the major prophets covered more ground while the minor prophets primarily dealt with specific subjects or issues regarding the nation.

Beginning with Isaiah through to the last book of the Old Testament, this section of the Scriptures is called the prophetic portion of the Bible. Prophets were men who were raised up by God during decadent times when both priests and kings were no longer worthy channels through which the expression of God might flow.

The qualifications of the prophet are given in Deuteronomy 18:20-22:

1.  True prophets rebuked sin in both high and low places.

2.  They warned the nation of what would happen if they didn't change their ways.

3.  They pleaded with the proud people to humble themselves and return to God. Fire and tears were mingled in their messages, which were not of doom and gloom alone, for they saw the Day of the Lord and the Glory to follow. All of them looked through the darkness to the dawn of a new day. In the night of sin, they saw the light of a coming Savior and Sovereign Lord. They saw the Millennial Kingdom coming in all its fullness. Their message must be interpreted before true appreciation of the Kingdom in the New Testament can be attained. The correct perspective of the Kingdom must be realized through the eyes of the Old Testament prophets.

## THE MAJOR PROPHETS

### THE BOOK OF ISAIAH

**Author:** *Isaiah (1:1)*

Chapter 6 records the personal call and commission of Isaiah. (This chapter seems as though it should be at the beginning of the book.)

Isaiah 36-39 is the historical section, which records the ministry of Isaiah during the crisis when the Assyrian host encompassed Jerusalem. Beyond these few personal sections, Isaiah stands in the shadows as he points to another who is to come: Christ.

**Theme:**

As the New Testament presents the Lord Jesus Christ as its theme, so Isaiah presents the Lord Jesus Christ as his book's theme: Christ's virgin birth, His character, His life, His death, His resurrection, and His second coming are presented in Isaiah with definitiveness and clarity (see I Peter 1:10-11, Luke 4:16-22, and Isaiah 61:1-4). Because of these thematic parallels, Bible scholar J. Vernon McGee has nicknamed Isaiah "the fifth gospel."

**Style and Content:**

The prophecy of Isaiah is also strikingly similar to the entire Bible, as can be seen in the following comparison. Notice that the 66 chapters of Isaiah represent the 66 books of the Bible:

| THE BIBLE | BOOK OF ISAIAH |
| --- | --- |
| 66 books | 66 chapters |
| 39 books in the Old Testament | 39 chapters on the Law and Government of God |
| 27 books in the New Testament | 27 chapters on the Grace and Salvation of God |

There are 66 direct quotations from Isaiah in the New Testament. Of the 27 New Testament books, 20 quote from Isaiah and 12 of these have direct quotations.

**Outline:**

Isaiah is divided into three sections:

1. *Judgment* (poetry)—Chapters 1-35: The revelation of the sovereign on the throne. Chapter 6 describes the government of God. Chapter 1 will break your heart when you see the breaking of God's heart.

2. *Historic Interlude*—Chapters 36-39: This section is probably a prophetic picture of how God will deliver His people during the Great Tribulation (see 2 Kings 18-19 and 2 Chronicles 29-30).

3. *Salvation* (poetry)—Chapters 40-66: The revelation of the Savior in the place of suffering. The Cross, chapter 53–the grace of God. The comfort of Jehovah through the Servant. Chapters 40-48: The salvation of Jehovah through the suffering Servant. Chapters 49-52:12: The glory of Jehovah through this suffering servant.

*Take time to enjoy Isaiah!* My favorite verses are 66:1-2 and 61:1-3. Isaiah is said to be the prophet of the Son (Jesus).

## THE BOOK OF JEREMIAH

**Author:** *Jeremiah, the prophet with the broken heart*

**His Life:**

This book is partly an autobiography, since he reveals so much of his personal history.

1. Born a priest in Anathoth, North of Jerusalem (1:1)

2. Chosen to be a prophet before he was born (1:5)

3. Called to the prophetic office while very young (1:6)

4. Commissioned (1:9-10).

5. Began his ministry during the reign of King Josiah and was a mourner at his funeral (2 Chronicles 35:25)

6. Forbidden to marry because of the terrible times (16:1-4)

7. Converted no one and was rejected by his people (11:18-21, 12:6, 18:17). Hated, beaten, and put in stocks (20:1-3). Imprisoned (37:11-16). Charged with being a traitor.

8. His message broke his own heart (9:1)

9. Wanted to resign but could not (20:9)

10. Saw the destruction of Jerusalem and the Babylonian captivity, was permitted to remain in the land by the captain of the Babylonian forces. He prophesied against the remnant to flee to Egypt (42:15, 43:3). Was forced to go with the remnant to Egypt (43:6-7). He died there; tradition says he was stoned by the remnant.

## His Personality:

God chose this man, who had a mother's heart, a trembling voice, and tear-filled eyes, to deliver a harsh message of judgment. The message that he gave broke his own heart. One author has written that "He was not a man mighty as Elijah, eloquent as Isaiah, or seraphic as Ezekiel, but one who was timid and shrinking, conscious of his helplessness, yearning for a sympathy and love he was never to know. Such was the chosen organ through which the Word of the Lord came to that corrupt and degenerate age."

The Lord Jesus Christ, weeping over Jerusalem, was a perfect fulfillment of Jeremiah.

**The Message:**

The message of Jeremiah was the most unwelcome ever delivered to a people. He was called a traitor because he said that they were to yield to Babylon (38:17-23). Isaiah, almost a century before him, had said to resist. In the economy of God, the nation was finished (15:1) and the time of the Gentiles had already begun with Babylon, the head of gold (Daniel 2). Jeremiah predicted the 70-year captivity in Babylon (25:9-12). However, he saw beyond the darkness to the light, and no prophet spoke so glowingly of the future as did he (23:3-8,31, 33:15-22).

**Key Word:** *Backsliding*

"Backsliding" occurs thirteen times—used only four other times in the Old Testament (Proverbs, once; Hosea, three times).

**Outline:**

Difficult to outline, because there is no logical or chronological order

1. Call of the prophet during the reign of Josiah, chapter 1

2. Prophesies to Judah and Jerusalem prior to Zedekiah's reign, Chapters 2-20

3. Judah is condemned because they have rejected Jehovah and created their own gods.

4. Prophesies during the reign of Zedekiah, chapters 21-29

5. Prophesies regarding the future of the 12 tribes and Judah's near captivity, chapters 30-39

6. Prophesies to the remnant who were left in the land after the destruction of Jerusalem, chapters 40-42

7. Prophesies during Jeremiah's last days in Egypt, chapters 43-51

8. Fulfillment of prophesied destruction of Jerusalem, chapter 52

Jeremiah is said to be the prophet of the Father (i.e., God the Father).

## THE BOOK OF LAMENTATIONS

**Author:** *Jeremiah*

This is a book of sorrow and pain, a poem of pity, a proverb of pathos, a hymn of heartbreak, a psalm of sadness, a symphony of sorrow. It is the wailing wall of the Bible.

**Key Verse:** *Lamentations 1:8*

It explains the reason that Jerusalem is in ruins. (Jerusalem has sinned gravely,Therefore she has become vile. All who honored her despise her because they have seen her nakedness; Yes, she sighs and turns away.)

**Features:**

- Jeremiah gazed upon the ruins of Jerusalem as it burned. Jesus later wept over the city because of what was going to happen.
- To Jeremiah, the destruction of the city was a matter of history, To Jesus, the destruction of the city was a matter of prophecy. The temple was destroyed after they rejected Jesus Christ.
- To Jeremiah, Jerusalem had sinned gravely; therefore she had become vile.

Chapter 5 ends with a cry to remember the nation Israel ("Jeremiah's Prayer"). As sad as this book is, we still see God's unfailing compassion and mercy with His love and faithfulness

## THE BOOK OF EZEKIEL

**Author:** *Ezekiel*

Ezekiel was a priest (Ezekiel 1:3) but never served in that office, as he was still a young man when he was taken during the reign of Jehoiachin (2 Kings 24:10-16). Daniel was taken captive in the first captivity during Jehoiakim's reign, about eight years before Ezekiel was taken captive.

Ezekiel was a contemporary of Jeremiah and Daniel. Jeremiah was an old man who spoke to the remnant that remained in the land; Daniel spoke in the court of the king of Babylon; Ezekiel spoke to the captives who had been brought to the rivers of Babylon. While the other captives wept when they remembered Zion, Ezekiel exulted in the greatest visions ever given to any prophet.

- **His Message:** Someone has said, "Ezekiel is the prophet of the Spirit, as Isaiah is the prophet of the Son, and Jeremiah the prophet of the Father." He warned the people that they must turn to God before they could return to Jerusalem.

- **His Method:** He warned against the false hope given by the false prophets and the indifference and the despondency begotten in the days of sin and disaster. Therefore, he resorted to a new method. Instead of *speaking* in parables, he acted them out (Ezekiel 24:24). We have had "flagpole sitters" and "walkathons" in our day, which attract the attention of the public.

This sort of thing was the method of Ezekiel and is indicative of a day of decay.

- **His Meaning:** Ezekiel was the prophet of the glory of the Lord. Three prophets of Israel spoke when they were out of the land: Ezekiel, Daniel, and John. Each wrote of an apocalypse. Although they used highly symbolic language, still they saw the brightest light and held the highest hope. Ezekiel looked beyond the sufferings of Christ to "the glories that would follow" (1 Peter 1:11).

**Outline:**

1. Glory of the Lord, Commission of the Prophet, Chapters 1-7

2. Glory of the Lord, complete captivity of Jerusalem and Israel; departure of the Glory, Chapters 8-24

3. Glory of the Lord; judgment of the nations, chapters 25-32

4. Glory of the Lord and coming of the kingdom, chapters 33-48

**Key Verses:** *Ezekiel 22:30; 33:11*

- "So I sought for a man among them who would make a wall, and stand in the gap before Me on behalf of the land, that I should not destroy it; but I found no one."

- "As I live," says the Lord GOD, "I have no pleasure in the death of the wicked, but that the wicked turn from his way and live. Turn, turn from your evil ways! For why should you die, O house of Israel?"

The saddest part of this book is when the Glory of the Lord departs from the temple (9:3, 10:4, and 10:18-19).

## THE BOOK OF DANIEL

**Author:** *Daniel*

Daniel gives a complete account of his life from the time he was carried away captive to Babylon until the first year of King Cyrus of Persia, which was about 536 BC (Daniel 9:2).

Daniel's life and ministry bridge the entire 70 years of captivity. At the beginning of the book, he is a boy in his teens; at the end of the book, he is an old man.

Here is God's estimate of Daniel: "Daniel, a man greatly beloved."

There are three words that characterize Daniel's life: Purpose, Prayer, and Prophecy. Daniel was a man of purpose (Daniel 1:8, 6:10). He was a man of prayer (2:17-23, 9:3-17). He was a man of prophecy (Matthew 24:15).

The book of Daniel gives the skeleton of prophecy upon which all prophecies are placed. Second Peter 1:20 ("...no prophecy of Scripture is of any private interpretation") and 2 Timothy 3:16-17 ("All Scripture is give by inspiration of God, and is profitable for doctrine, for reproof, for correction, for instruction in righteousness, that the man of God may be complete, thoroughly equipped for every good work.")

**Date:**

From the third year of the king of Babylon to about 606 BC, Daniel 1:1 and the first year of King Cyrus of Persia, 536 BC, Daniel 1:21.

**Theme:**

Daniel 2:44 – "And in the days of these kings the God of heaven will set up a kingdom which shall never be destroyed; and the kingdom shall not be left to other people; it shall break in pieces and consume all these kingdoms, and it shall stand forever."

**Outline:**

1. Historic night with prophetic light, chapters 1-6

   - A) Fall of Jerusalem, the dream and decree of the King of Babylon

   - B) Fall of Babylon and the decree of Darius, king of Medo-Persia

2. Prophetic light in historic night, chapters 7-12.
   Daniel's four visions and Daniel's prayer, chapter 9:1-19 (one of my favorite prayers)

## ENTER THE MINOR PROPHETS

BEGINNING with Hosea and concluding with Malachi, there are 12 short prophecies called the minor prophecies, not because of the message but the size of the book.

Rulers and priests were corrupted, and God decided to raise prophets for Himself to communicate with them to warn the people.

### THE BOOK OF HOSEA

**Author:**

Hosea. All that is known of him is what he reveals in his prophecy.

**Timeline:**

Hosea 1:1. In spite of the fact that Hosea mentions the four kings of Judah first and the one king of Israel last, he was the prophet of the Northern Kingdom, as the content of the book reveals. He was a contemporary with Amos, another prophet to Israel and also contemporary with Micah and Isaiah, prophets to Judah. His ministry extended over a-half century, and he lived to see the fulfillment of his prophecy in the captivity of Israel.

**Theme:**

Return to the Lord (Hosea 6:1) Backsliding was the sin of the people. What Jeremiah was to Judah at the time of the captivity of the Southern Kingdom, Hosea was to Israel more than a century before, at the time the captivity of Northern Kingdom (Israel). Both speak of heartbreaking personal experience.

**Personal experience:**

Hosea's experience was in the home, while Jeremiah's was in the nation. Jeremiah was commanded not to marry, while Hosea was commanded to marry a harlot, as he brutally stated: "a wife of whoredom." Her name was Gomer, and she bore him two sons and a daughter and then returns to her harlotry. Hosea puts her out of his house, but God commands him to go and take this unfaithful wife and bring her back to his house to love her again. God said in effect to Hosea, "Now you are prepared to speak for me to Israel, for Israel played the harlot. But I love her and will yet bring her back again into her Homeland."

**Outline:**

1. *Personal*. The prophet and his faithless wife, chapters 1-3

2. *Prophetic*. The Lord and the faithless nation (Israel), chapters 4-14. Israel will return to the land in the last days and will be saved in the future.

**Key verse:**

Hosea 11:8 (powerful verse—God's heart is laid bare): "How can I give you up, Ephraim? How can I hand you over, Israel? How can I make you like Admah? How can I set you like Zeboiim? My heart churns within Me; My sympathy is stirred.

**My favorite Verse:** *Hosea 14:4*

---

*O Israel, return to the LORD your God, For you have stumbled because of your iniquity.*

---

## THE BOOK OF JOEL

**Author:** *Joel*

Nothing is known of this prophet except what is given in the opening. His name means "Jehovah is God."

**Date:** *About the time of the reign of Joash*

Considered by many to be the earliest of the writing prophets, Joel was a prophet to Judah probably about the time of the reign of Joash king of Judah. It is likely that he knew Elijah and Elisha.

**Theme:** *The Day of the Lord*

The Day of the Lord, chapters 1:15, 2:1-11, 31 and 3:14.

**Features:**

The Day of the Lord, or the day of Jehovah, is an expression introduced by Joel ( if he is the first of writing prophets, he saw the furthest into the future).

"The Day of the Lord" is an expression loaded with meaning. It seems to include not only the coming millennial kingdom, but also includes all the judgment that precedes the setting up of the Kingdom and the return of Christ.

His description of a literal plague of locusts and its comparison with future judgment is a dramatic and literary gem.

He is the prophet who introduces the outpouring of the Holy Spirit that was referred to by Peter in the day of Pentecost in the book of Acts.

**Outline:**

1.  Literal and local plague of locusts, 1:1-14

2.  Looking *to* the day of the Lord, 1:15-2:32 (prelude)

3.  Looking *at* the day of the Lord, chapter 3 (postlude)

    a. The Great Tribulation, chapter 3:1-15

    b. The Millennial Kingdom in view, chapter 3:16-21

My favorite verse is 2:32. Chapter 3:12-14 corresponds with Revelation 14:17-20.

## THE BOOK OF AMOS

**Author:** *Amos*

Amos was not a graduate of the school of prophets, but was a layman. He was also a herdsman and a gatherer of sycamore fruit (chapter 1:1, 7:14-15. He was a native Takoa chapter 1:1, a village about 12 miles south of Jerusalem. Although born in Judah, his messages were to the northern kingdom of Israel primarily and to the world in general.

**Timeline:** *During the Reign of Jeroboam*

His ministry was during the Reign of Jeroboam, the second king of the Northern Kingdom and Uzziah, king of Judah

**Theme:** *God is the Ruler of the world*

He declares that God is the Ruler of the world and that the nations were responsible to Him. The measure of responsibility for every nation is determined upon the light that each nation has received. The final test for any nation or individual is found in Amos 3:3: "Can two walk together, except they agree?"

In a day of prosperity, Amos pronounced God's punishment. The judgment of God awaited those nations living in luxury and steeped in immorality.

**Outline:**

1. Amos 1:1-2:3: Judgment on the surrounding nations

2. Amos 2:4 – 6:14: Judgment on Judah and Israel

3. Amos 7-9: Visions of the future regathering and restoration of Israel's kingdom

## THE BOOK OF OBADIAH

**Author:** *Obadiah*

Obadiah's name means "servant of Jehovah." Not much is known about him. He is somewhat like ghostwriter; he is there, but we don't know him. Obadiah lived up to his name, "Servant." God has willed that his name and this prophecy should be known to the world.

**Date:** *Undetermined*

Obadiah could have been written during Babylon's captivity.

**Key word:**

Edom. This book is the prophecy of judgment against Edom. The Edomites were descendants of Esau, while the Israelites were the descendants of Jacob (the two sons of Isaac and Rebekah—Genesis 25:24-34. In Malachi 1:2-3, God says, "Jacob I loved and Esau I hated." The explanation for that is given in this book.

**Outline:**

1.  Edom's destruction verses 1-16.

2.  Israel's restoration verses 17-21.

Edom was judged for his cruelty toward his brother Jacob (Israel).

## THE BOOK OF JONAH

**Author:** *Jonah*

This book does not seem to be a prophecy but the actual experience of the prophet.

**Date:** *Around 750 BC*

Written about 750 BC, when Nineveh was at the height of its glory. It is said to have been destroyed by 606 BC. Our Lord Jesus considered Jonah a real person, and He accepted the record of Jonah as true (Luke 11:30 and Matthew 12:39-41).

**Comments:**

The fish is *not* the hero of the story! The essential characters are Jehovah and Jonah (i.e., God and man).

**Significant subjects:**

- This is one book of the Old Testament that sets forth the Resurrection.

- Salvation is not by works (chapter 2:9). Salvation is of the Lord.

- God's grace and purposes cannot be frustrated. This book shows God's determination to get His message of salvation to people who will hear and receive it.

- God will not cast us aside for our faithlessness! When Jonah failed the first time, God didn't give him up. Some of the most encouraging words that a faltering child of God can hear are "…and the word of the Lord came to Jonah the second time (Jonah 3:1).

- God is good and gracious. The penetrating picture of God throughout the entire Bible is portrayed in Jonah 3:2. God is not a vengeful Deity in the book of Jonah. Personally speaking, Jonah 4:2 touches me deeply, for it shows the character and the heart of our beloved God. It will bless you to know this verse.

- God is the God of the Gentiles as well as the God of the Jews. It has been suggested that Romans 3:29 might well be inscribed above the name of this book: "Or is He the God of the Jews only? Is He not also the God of the Gentiles? Yes, of the Gentiles also…"

- The book of Jonah is a great book on missions and has a vision for the world in view.

Notice the striking resemblance between Jonah and the Apostle Paul. Both were missionaries to the Gentiles, both were shipwrecked, both were witnesses to the sailors on board, both were used to deliver these sailors from death.

**Outline:**

The four chapters of the book of Jonah may be divided into four missionary journeys:

1.  Into the fish

2.  Onto dry land

3.  On to Nineveh

4.  Into the heart of God

## THE BOOK OF MICAH

**Author:** *Micah*

Micah's name means "who is like Jehovah?" He was an inhabitant of Moresheth (Micah 1:1; 14), which was located about 20 miles Southwest of Jerusalem.

**Date:** *Eighth Century BC (shortly before the fall of Samaria in 722/21 BC)*

Micah was younger than Isaiah, and his prophecy is called a miniature or shorthand version of Isaiah. His ministry is directed at both Jerusalem and Samaria and witnessed the captivity of the Northern Kingdom.

**Theme:**

The judgment and redemption of God. Micah 7:18 tells us that God hates sin but loves the souls of sinners.

**Remarks:**

Micah's style is touching and tender, and there is exquisite beauty about this book, which combines God's infinite tenderness with His judgment. This prophet saw clearly the coming redemption of Israel.

Micah condemns violence, corruption, robbery, covetousness, gross materialism, and spiritual bankruptcy. He could well be labeled "the Prophet of the City." He pronounced judgment on the cities of Israel and on Jerusalem in Judah with their urban problems.

**Outline:**

Micah gave three messages, each beginning with the injunction for them to "hear," (Micah 1:2, 3:1, and 6:1). The first was addressed to all people. The second was addressed specifically to the leaders of Israel. The third was a personal word, pleading with Israel to repent and return to God, a] Proclaiming the future judgment for past sins, chapters 1-3. b) Prophesying future Glory, because of His past promises, chapters 4-5. c) Pleading for present repentance because of past redemption. chapter 6. d) Pardoning all iniquity because of who God is and what He does, chapter 7.

**My favorite verse:** *Micah 6:8*

---

*He has shown you, O man, what is good;*
*And what does the LORD require of you*
*But to do justly,*
*To love mercy,*
*And to walk humbly with your God?*

---

## THE BOOK OF NAHUM

**Author:** *Nahum*

Nahum means "Comforter." He is identified in Nahum 1:1 as an Elkoshite. This is all that is known of him. Elkosh was most likely a village in Galilee.

**Date:** *720–636 BC*

About 100 years after Jonah and about 100 years before the destruction of Nineveh, which took place in 612 BC.

**Theme:**

The burden, or judgment, of Nineveh (v.1:1)

**Message:**

Nearly a century before, Jonah had brought a message from God to these people, and Nineveh had repented. Sadly, however, the repentance was not permanent, and still, God patiently gave this new generation an opportunity to repent. In Nahum 1:3, finally, the day of Grace ends, and the moment of doom has arrived (3:19). This is a message of comfort to a people who had lived under fear in a powerful and Godless nation. Eventually, God will destroy any Godless nation, a fact that reveals the other side of the attributes of God. God is Love. He is also Holy, Righteous, and Good.

**Outline:**

1.  Nahum 1:1-8: The justice and goodness of God

2.  Nahum 1:9-15: The justice and goodness of God demonstrated in His decision to destroy Nineveh and to proclaim the Gospel.

3.  Nahum 2-3: The avenging action of God justified.

**My favorite verse:** *Nahum 1:7*

> *The LORD is good,*
> *A stronghold in the day of trouble;*
> *And He knows those who trust in Him.*

## THE BOOK OF HABAKKUK

**Author:** *Habakkuk*

Habakkuk means "Love's Embrace." Habakkuk embraces his people and takes them into his arms, much as one embraces a weeping child to quiet it with the assurance that if God wills, it shall soon be better. Some say that Habakkuk is the Old Testament story of a "doubting Thomas," who seemed to have a question mark for a brain.

**Date:** *Late Seventh Century BC (c. 626 to 605 BC)*

Habakkuk was probably written during the reign of Josiah around the time of the destruction of Nineveh and the rise of Babylon to power. He appeared in the twilight, historically speaking, just before the darkness of the captivity.

**Message:**

The book opens in gloom and ends in Glory. It begins with a question mark and closes with an exclamation point. Why God permits evil is a question that every thoughtful mind has faced and the book of Habakkuk answers these questions. Is God doing anything about the wrongs of the world? Will He straighten out the injustice of the world? This book says that He is and He will. This book is written from the prophet's personal experience described in poetry.

**Theme:** *Faith*

Habakkuk has been called the prophet of faith. Habakkuk 2:4, "The just shall live by faith," is quoted three times in the New Testament: Romans 1:17, Galatians 3:11, and Hebrews 10:38.

**Outline:**

- Chapter 1: The *perplexity* of the prophet
- Chapter 2: The *perspicuity* of the prophet
- Chapter 3: The *pleasure* of the prophet

The book ends with a hymn of faith in 3:17-19. Habakkuk has moved from pain to pleasure.

This also is my personal hymn of faith, for I have faced many perplexities in life, and this book comforts me again and again.

## THE BOOK OF ZEPHANIAH

**Author:** *Zephaniah*

Zephaniah traced his lineage back to his great-great-grandfather, who was Hezekiah, king of Judah. Thus, Zephaniah was of the royal line.

**Date:** *c. 635 to 625 BC*

The author places the time of his writing during the days of Josiah, the king of Judah in Zephaniah 1:1. According to the arrangement of the Hebrew Scriptures, Zephaniah was the last of the prophets before Israel went into captivity. He was a contemporary of Jeremiah and probably with Micah. This book is the "swan song" of the Davidic kingdom. Zephaniah is credited with giving impetus to the revival that took place during the reign of Josiah.

**Theme:**

The dark side of love. God is judging the people because He is a *just* God. He is displaying His mercy because He loves. How amazing it is that even when He judges, it is an act of His love and mercy!

**Remarks:**

1. The phrase "the Day of the Lord" (indicating the time of God's wrath) occurs seven times (i.e., the Great Tribulation).

2. "Jealousy" occurs twice. It is not on the same level as human jealousy but reveals the love of God for His people who have failed.

**Outline:**

1. Chapter 1: The judgment of Judah and Jerusalem

2. Chapter 2:1-3:8: The judgment of the earth and all of the nations chapter 2:1- 3:8

3. Chapter 3:9-20: All judgment is removed; the Kingdom is established

**My favorite verse:** *Zephaniah 3:17*

---

*"The LORD your God in your midst,*
*The Mighty One, will save;*
*He will rejoice over you with gladness,*
*He will quiet you with His love,*
*He will rejoice over you with singing."*

---

It reminds me over and over again of God's infinite love for me even when I fail. It is Glorious!

The prophets who prophesied to the returned remnant were Haggai, Zachariah, and Malachi.

## THE BOOK OF HAGGAI

**Author:**

Haggai was one of the two prophets who encouraged the Remnant who had returned to Israel after the Babylonian captivity to rebuild the Temple. In Haggai's prophecy, four things about this man are apparent:

1.  He was self-effacing. He exalted the Lord

2.  He was God's messenger ("Thus says the Lord").

3.  He not only rebuilt, but he also cheered and encouraged the people.

4.  He not only preached, he practiced.

**Date:** *520 BC*

**Theme:** *The Temple*

Rebuilding the Temple was the supreme passion of this prophet. He not only rebuked the people for their delay in rebuilding the Temple but he also encouraged and helped them, because he was a down-to-earth, practical prophet who put his faith into action. The prophecy of Haggai and the epistle of James have much in common. Both put the emphasis upon the daily grind.

**Outline:**

1.  Chapter 1:1-11: A challenge to the people

2.  Chapter 1:12-15: The people's response to the challenge

3.  Chapter 2:1-9: The discouragement of the people and the encouragement from the Lord

4. Chapter 2:10-19: An appeal to the Law, and an explanation of the principle chapter

5. Chapter 2:20-23: The revelation of God's program and expectation for the future

**Key passage:** *Haggai 1:8-9*

---

*"Go up to the mountains and bring wood and build the temple, that I may take pleasure in it and be glorified," says the LORD. You looked for much, but indeed it came to little; and when you brought it home, I blew it away. Why?" says the LORD of hosts. "Because of My house that is in ruins, while every one of you runs to his own house."*

---

These two verses touch me deeply. How many times we neglect our Lord while we take care of Number one (ourselves)!

## THE BOOK OF ZECHARIAH

**Author:** *Zechariah*

Zechariah, whose name means "Whom Jehovah remembers," is identified in Zechariah 1:1 as the son of Berechiah (which means "Jehovah blesses") and his father was the son of Iddo, which means "the appointed time." When you put these three names together, they indicate that God remembers and blesses in the appointed time. Zechariah was sent as encouragement for the Remnant.

**Date:** *520 BC*

**Characteristics:**

Zechariah was born outside of Israel, but he wrote this book inside of Israel. He includes more Messianic prophecies than any of the minor prophets.

**Outline:**

1. Chapters 1-6: Apocalyptic visions (Messianic and Millennial) 1-6

2. Chapters 7-8: Historic Interlude. A question arises concerning the religious ritual of fasting in Zechariah 7:1-3. The three-fold answer is given:

   - a. When the heart is right, the ritual is right (7:4-7).
   - b. When the heart is wrong, the ritual is wrong (7:8-14).
   - c. God's purpose concerning Jerusalem is unmoved by any religious rituals (8:1-23).

3. Prophetic Burdens (Zechariah 9-14)

   - a. Connected with the First Coming of Christ (chapters 9-11)
   - b. Connected with Second Coming of Christ (chapters 12-14).

**My favorite verses:**

- Zechariah 9:9—First coming of Christ.
- Zechariah 14:16-21—Second coming of Christ.

## THE BOOK OF MALACHI

**Author:** *Malachi*

Malachi means "My Messenger."

**Date:** *Probably 397 BC*

Malachi concluded the Books of the Prophets as Nehemiah concluded the Books of the Historians. He prophesied either during the latter period of Nehemiah's governorship or immediately after it.

**Message:**

The message gives three references:

1. He referred to Levi as the "messenger [i.e., angel] of the Lord," which indicates that every believer of God is an "angel" of the Lord (Malachi 2:7).

2. He announced the coming of John the Baptist as "my messenger" in Malachi 3:1. John the Baptist was the "Malachi" of the New Testament and began where Malachi of the Old Testament left off.

3. Malachi also made a definite reference to Christ as the messenger of the new covenant in Malachi 3:1.

Malachi begins with God's declaration to or interrogation of Israel, and then He gives Israel's answer, which is sophisticated sarcasm. Finally, He gives God's reply, which is actually biting sarcasm.

Malachi's prophecy reveals an age when people have become deadened to sin. Either they were "drugged" to an unconsciousness of sin, or they were in a spiritual stupor, with no conviction of sin. That is the worst place to be! They mouthed surprise that God would find fault with them. They pretended to know everything but were woefully lacking in a knowledge of essentials.

**Outline:**

1. Chapter 1:1-5—Describes the Love of God for Israel

2. Chapter 1:6-2:9—The priest is reproved for profanity

3. Chapter 2:10-17—The people are rebuked for social sin

4. Chapter 3:1-6—The prediction of the two messengers to come

5. Chapter 3:7-18—The people are rebuked for their religious sin

6. Chapter 4:1-6—The prediction of the Day of the Lord and the sun of Righteousness who ushers it in

**Key Verses:** *Malachi 3:1, 4:2*

*"Behold, I send My messenger,*
And he will prepare the way before Me
And the LORD, whom you seek,
Will suddenly come to His temple,
Even the Messenger of the covenant,
In whom you delight.
Behold, He is coming,"
Says the LORD of hosts.

*But to you who fear My name*
The Sun of Righteousness shall arise
With healing in His wings;
And you shall go out
And grow fat like stall-fed calves.

# chapter twelve

# Introducing the New Testament: The Four Gospels

**Introduction:**

THE OLD TESTAMENT becomes a reality in the New Testament. There are approximately 400 years that take place between the days of Malachi and the birth of JESUS CHRIST.

This is a great yawning chasm of silence as far as the Scriptures are concerned. God is in the shadows and remains silent during this period. Nevertheless, this was a thrilling time, when world-shaking events were transpiring. The Medo-Persian Empire was in power during the life of Malachi.

Medo-Persia is no longer. World power shifted from the East to the West, from Asia to Europe, and from Medo-Persia to the Grecian Empire, which was swallowed up by the Roman Empire. Meanwhile, the nation of Israel (or the nation of Judah) turned away from idolatry after the Babylonian captivity and thus began a frantic striving for legalistic holiness. The Law became an idol to them. The Synagogue was the center of their life in Judah and everywhere else they went in the world.

There were four political entities:

1. *Pharisees* — These were the defenders of the Jewish way of life against all foreign influences. They were strict legalists who believed in the Old Testament and, politically, were nationalistic. They embraced the supernatural.

2. *Sadducees* — Wealthy, socially minded, and wanting to get rid of traditions, they rejected the supernatural. They may have been what today we would call "progressive."

3. *Scribes* — A group of professional expounders of the Law who had stemmed from the days of Ezra. They became hair-splitters of the Law and were more concerned with the *letter* of the Law than the *spirit* of the Law.

4. *Herodians* — Political opportunists who sought to keep Herod on the throne.

Although this period is marked by the silence of God, it is nevertheless evident that God was preparing the world for the coming of CHRIST. The Jewish people, the Greek civilization, the Roman Empire, and the seething multitudes of the Orient were being prepared for the coming of a Savior, insomuch that these events produced the scene that the Apostle Paul labeled "the fullness of time" (Galatians 4:4).

AD (*Anno Domini*)— "In the Year of the Lord" JESUS was born in Bethlehem, the city of David.

**Overview of the Gospels:**

- Matthew emphasizes that Jesus is the Messiah and the king of the Jews: He is a Lion.
- Mark emphasizes that that Jesus is the Servant of Jehovah: "Jesus came." He is an Ox.
- Luke emphasizes that Jesus is the Perfect man, the second and the last Adam: He is a Man.
- John emphasizes that Jesus is God: "God became a man." He is an Eagle.
- In Matthew, He is the king. Matthew wrote for the Jews. The *Kingdom* is the focus.
- In Mark, He is the Servant. Mark wrote for the Romans. *Service* is the focus.
- In Luke, Jesus is the perfect Man. Luke wrote for the Greeks. *Perfection* is the Focus.
- In John, He is God. John wrote for Humanity, presenting Jesus as the Savior of the world. *God became a man*!

## THE GOSPEL OF MATTHEW

**Author:** *Matthew*

Matthew was a converted tax collector who was chosen to write to the Jews concerning their Messiah. The Gospel stands like a swinging door between the two Testaments. It swings back into the Old Testament, gathering up prophecies that were fulfilled at the first coming of Christ and swings forward into the new Testament, speaking of the new creation of God: " On this rock I will build My church," Jesus said in Matthew 16:18.

The time period extends from Abraham in the Old Testament to Joseph, the husband of Mary, thus establishing Jesus as the heir to the Kingdom.

**Outline:**

1.  Behold your King: the Person of the King, Matthew 1-2

2.  Preparation for and of the King, Matthew 3-4:16

3.  Presentation of the King, Matthew 4:17- 9:35

4.  Program of the King, Matthew 9:36 – 16:20

5.  Passion of the King, Matthew 16:21 – 27:66

6.  Power of the King, Matthew 28

**Key Verses:**

It is difficult to choose a key verse, but it is important to meditate on the following verses because they clearly identify Jesus as the King of the whole world, especially to the Jewish people.

- Matthew 1:23 — *"Behold, the virgin shall be with child, and bear a Son, and they shall call His name Immanuel," which is translated, "God with us."*

- Matthew 3:17 — *"And suddenly a voice came from heaven, saying, 'This is My beloved Son, in whom I am well pleased.'"*

- Matthew 6:33 — *"But seek first the kingdom of God and His righteousness, and all these things shall be added to you."*

- Matthew 11:28-30 — *"Come to Me, all you who labor and are heavy laden, and I will give you rest. Take My yoke upon you and learn from Me, for I am gentle and lowly in heart, and you will find rest for your souls. For My yoke is easy and My burden is light."*

- Matthew 28:18-20 — *"And Jesus came and spoke to them, saying, 'All authority has been given to Me in heaven and on earth. Go therefore and make disciples of all the nations, baptizing them in the name of the Father and of the Son and of the Holy Spirit, teaching them to observe all things that I have commanded you; and lo, I am with you always, even to the end of the age.' Amen."*

- Matthew 5, 6, and 7, called the Sermon on the Mount, elevates holiness to a prime new paradigm. Jesus takes the Law, which requires action on our part, and drives it deep inside of us to reveal our hearts. He examines our thoughts and motives before we even act upon them, and we are indicted. But actually, if you look closely, Jesus is not asking us to do better but is beckoning us to come to Him—once we realize our colossal failure to keep the Law—with broken hearts and contrite spirits.

**Remarks:**

The Gospel of Matthew: Jesus is presented as a King. This book was written for the Jews.

I love this Gospel because Jesus clearly states who He is and presents a wonderful new way of life under a New Covenant and under a new Kingdom. He shows us how our relationship with God and with each other is supposed to look. This is also a beautiful picture of the Cross.

**Favorite passage:** *Matthew 11:28-30*

## THE GOSPEL OF MARK

**Author:** *Mark*

**Date:** *c. AD 63*

Mark's mother was a prominent Jewish Christian in the Jerusalem church. Mark was the cousin of Barnabas (Colossians 4:10).

**Theme:** *Two important phrases*

1. "The beginning of the Gospel of Jesus" (v. 1)

2. "Jesus came" (vv 9, 14)

Mark opens this book with the words, "The beginning of the gospel of Jesus Christ...." This is a Gospel of *action*. He begins with the baptism of Jesus, His temptation, and His ministry in Galilee. He does not start with the beginning of *Jesus* Himself but with the *work* of Jesus. Mark's is the "Gospel of Miracles." Jesus is presented as the Servant of Jehovah (Isaiah 42:1-2).

**Keywords:** *"Jesus came" and "Immediately"*

**Key verse:** *Mark 10:45*

As mentioned above, this is a gospel of action and accomplishments. It was mainly written for Romans. They were a busy people who believed in power and action. In this book, Jesus is stripped and girded for action. It is written in the language of the common people. Jesus came in the winsomeness of His humanity and in the fullness of His Deity, doing good. This was only the beginning of the Gospel. Jesus died, He arose from the grave, and then He said to His own, "Go into all the world...." At that point, the Gospel account by Mark was completed. This is the Gospel today.

**Outline:** *The credentials of Christ as "the Servant"*

1. John the Baptist *introduces* the Servant (Mark 1:1-8)

2. God *identifies* the Servant (Mark 1:9-11 and 9:1-8) in the Transfiguration

3. The temptation of Jesus *initiates* the Servant chapter (Mark 1:12-13)

4. The works and the words serve to *illustrate* the Servant chapters (1:14 -13:37)

5. The Death, Burial, and Resurrection *insure* the Servant chapters (14:1-16:20)

My favorite verse is Mark 13:11, and even though I have not been arrested for the sake of the Gospel yet, this verse is a reality in my daily life again and again.

## THE GOSPEL OF LUKE

**Author:** *Luke*

**Date:** *Probably the last Synoptic Gospel written, preceding the book of Acts*

A beloved Gentile physician (Colossians 4:14), Luke was the only Gentile who contributed to the writing of the Gospel and to the whole Bible, for that matter. He also wrote the book of The Acts of the Apostles. He was a beloved physician and a loyal friend of the Apostle Paul. Both Paul and Luke were highly intellectual and familiar with the Greek culture and language. (Perhaps this is the reason why they were such a good friends and brothers in the Lord.)

Luke writes this Gospel from Mary's point of view and gives a more detailed genealogy of Jesus than any of the other Gospel writers. He begins with Jesus and goes back all the way to Adam, the son of God (Luke 3:23-38). Jesus came through Nathan, the son of David, in Mary's genealogy, which traces the bloodline to David. And in Matthew he connects the royal line through Joseph, Mary's husband.

The choice of Luke by the Holy Spirit to write the third Gospel reveals that there are no accidental writers of Scripture. The selection of Luke was supernatural. He was a physician and a scientist in his day. He was a better Greek writer than any of the New Testament authors, including Paul. Luke was a careful and accurate historian with remarkable ability for detail.

**Theme:** *"Behold the Man."*

Jesus is called "the second man" but "the last Adam" (1 Corinthians 15:45-47). God is helping men to become like Jesus (1 John 3:2), and therefore, Jesus is the called the second man. Out of Him will come many sons of God: "the Church." He is the "last Adam," and there will not be another head of the human family. He succeeds where Adam failed. Adam "became a living soul," whereas Jesus is a life-giving Spirit.

Jesus was made like His brothers that His brothers might become like Him (Hebrews 2:17).

The Song of Mary is found in Luke's gospel. He gives more details regarding John the Baptist's birth and message, Christ's birth, the angels singing, Christ's birth being announced to Mary, heaven and earth exulting together at the announcement of the Savior, about Mary, Elizabeth, John the Baptist, and Zechariah the priest all being filled with the Spirit.

**Outline:**

1.  Birth of the perfect Man and His family (Luke 1-3)

2.  The testing of the perfect Man by Satan and His rejection by His hometown (Luke 4)

3.  Ministry of the perfect Man (Luke 5-21)

4.  Betrayal, trial, and death of the perfect Man (Luke 22-23)

5.  Resurrection of the perfect Man (Luke 24)

Luke tells us of twenty miracles, and six of these are not recorded in any other Gospels. Luke's account of the virgin birth is the most detailed. He gives twenty-three parables, and eighteen of them are found nowhere else, e.g., the parables of the prodigal son and the good Samaritan. He also gives us the very human account of our resurrected Lord's walk on the road to Emmaus, which proves that Jesus was still human after His resurrection.

In the Gospel of Luke, my Jesus is the Perfect Man.

**My favorite verses:**

Luke 1: 77-79 and the song of Mary in chapter 1:46-55 rock me every time.

## THE GOSPEL OF JOHN

**Author:** *John*

John was an Apostle, the Son of Zebedee and Salome, and the brother of James (Mark 1:19-20, John 21:20-24).

**Theme:** *God became a man.*

**Date:** *c. AD 90-100*

The Gospel of John, the three Letters of John, and the Book of Revelation were evidently written during the last ten years of the life of the beloved apostle. Even though it is hard to choose one Gospel out the four Gospels (because each gives a compelling revelation of our Lord), the Gospel of John walks into my heart with wooden shoes. This is where the Deity of Christ, along with his humanity, gloriously and harmoniously converge in this beautiful tapestry. It is one of my favorite books.

In this book, our Lord is the True Good Shepherd. He is "the way, the Truth, and the Life." He is the Bread of Life. He is the Living Water. He is the True Vine. He is the Light of the World.

**Outline:**

1. Chapters 1-12—*Light*

2. Chapters 13-17—*Love*

3. Chapters 18-21—*Life*

**Highlights:**

- John 1:1-18 sets the *tone* for the whole book: Who is Jesus?
- John 3: 16-17 gives the *purpose* of the book. (Chapter 17 gets me every time! His heart is bared, and oh, how He loves me!)
- John 19: Jesus goes to the Cross in my place. Verse 30, His last words: "IT IS FINISHED." I can hear the Father's response, "SATISFIED! Justice and Mercy have kissed."
- John 20:30: So that you may believe.
- The book ends with John 21:25: "There are also many other things that Jesus did, which if they were written one by one, I suppose that even the world itself could not contain the books that would be written."

*Amen.*

# chapter thirteen

# A New Nation Is Born: Church History in the New Testament

WE ENTER INTO a prime new section of the Bible. Up to this point in history, the world was divided into two groups, the Jews and the Gentiles. Now a new nation is born from the two – "the church of Jesus Christ." It is composed of Jews *and* Gentiles. A new nationality, new citizens, a new country—they called themselves Pilgrims, and Heaven is their home.

It all began with 120 people huddled fearfully together in an upper room in Jerusalem waiting for further instructions from the Lord and the promise of the Holy Spirit, as Jesus had told them. Before His resurrection, as we saw in the Gospels, Jesus was still operating under the Old Testament law. After His Resurrection, the New Covenant began.

In the Book of Acts, we see that the promise of the Holy Spirit, spoken of in Luke 24:49, has come, and the world has been forever changed. What had consisted of a handful of fearful disciples in Jerusalem eventually became a worldwide movement that turned the world upside down—or, shall I say, "right side up?" The Church Age had begun. It is the age of Grace, when "Love came down," and it is still going on today. We now live in "the age of the Holy Spirit."

God the Holy Spirit, who in the former times came upon individuals so that they could do His work and minister to people, now makes His permanent home in the hearts of those who believe in and receive Him through the Lord Jesus Christ. Our hearts are now the new "temple." The plan of God, which began before the foundation of the world, has become a reality. God the Father purposed it. God the Son performed it. God the Holy Spirit protects it.

*God chose us.*
*Jesus redeemed us.*
*The Holy Spirit sealed us.*

## THE BOOK OF THE ACTS OF THE APOSTLES

This book is sometimes called the fifth Gospel, and while the other four Gospels are part of the Old Covenant, the Book of the Acts of the Apostles ushers in a new covenant called the New Testament. Since then, both Jews and Gentiles can come to God only through Jesus Christ and Him alone, as He says in John 14:6: "I Am the way, the Truth, and the Life; no one comes to the Father except through Me."

The Book of Acts is, in a way, a continuation of the Gospel of Luke. It contains the last recorded facts about Jesus. Acts brings all four Gospels together. The great missionary commission given in the four Gospels is confirmed in Acts. Matthew told us of the Resurrection; Mark, the Ascension; Luke, the promise of the Holy Spirit, and John, the Promise of the Second Coming.

The Book of Acts furnishes a ladder on which to place the Epistles and serves as the bridge between the Gospels and the Epistles.

**Author:** *Luke*

**Date:** *c. AD 63*

This book covers approximately thirty years. It is the inspired record of the beginning of the church. Although Genesis recorded the origin of the physical universe, Acts records the origin of the spiritual body.

**Key verse:** *1:8*

**Outline:**

1. The Lord Jesus is at work by the Holy Spirit through the Apostles in Jerusalem, chapters 1-7.

2. The Lord Jesus is at work by the Holy Spirit through the Apostles in Judea and Samaria, chapters 8-12.

3. The Lord Jesus is at work by the Holy Spirit through the Apostles to the outermost part of the earth, chapters13-28.

A new nation, in which you and I have a part, is born and is being added to every day. The Book of Acts ushers in the Church Age. "Therefore old things have passed away; behold, all things have become new" (2 Corinthians 5:17).

It's a new beginning for mankind—a new covenant with God, a new Tabernacle, which is now in our hearts! This new nation is the Temple of the Holy Spirit corporately, and individually we are "a new Creation." This amazing gift is further expanded and explained in the Epistles. The Apostle Paul first appears in the book of Acts as a prosecutor and destroyer of the church and the Gospel. He later becomes a great advocate for the Gospel and a restorer of the church of his beloved Christ.

The book of Acts is about the introduction and the works of the third Person of the Godhead, the Holy Spirit. I love this Book! He is bold and active.

**The Holy Spirit:**

*Wind—He disturbs our complacency.*
*Fire—He cleanses and purifies us.*
*Water—He gives us life.*

**Favorite verse:** *Acts 1:8*

---

*But you shall receive power when the Holy Spirit has come upon you; and you shall be witnesses to Me in Jerusalem, and in all Judea and Samaria, and to the end of the earth.*

---

*Amen.*

# chapter fourteen

# The Epistles of the New Testament

THE EPISTLES are letters that were written by holy men of God as they were moved by the Holy Spirit and are intended for the edification of the Church.

**Purpose:**

To build and strengthen the body of Christ, which is the Church. "All scripture is given by the inspiration of God and is profitable for doctrine, for reproof, for correction, for instruction in Righteousness that the man of God may be complete, thoroughly equipped for every good work" (2 Timothy 3:16-17).

# THE PAULINE EPISTLES
### Romans, First & Second Corinthians, Galatians

## THE BOOK OF ROMANS

**Author:** *Paul*

**Date:** *AD 57- 58 (during Paul's third missionary journey)*

**Location:** *Corinth*

**Subject:** *The RIGHTEOUSNESS of GOD*

The Book of Romans contains the great "Gospel Manifesto" for the world. To Paul, the Gospel was the great ecumenical movement, and Rome was the center of the world for which Christ had died.

The Book of Romans is an eloquent and passionate declaration of the Gospel of Jesus Christ by a man who made an arduous but productive journey to die for Christ, the One who had died for him. The Book of Romans is more than mere cold logic. It is in fact the Gospel presented in warm love.

**Key passage:** *Romans 1:16-17*

"For I am not ashamed of the gospel of Christ, for it is the power of God to salvation for everyone who believes, for the Jew first and also for the Greek. For in it the righteousness of God is revealed from faith to faith; as it is written, *'The just shall live by faith.'*"

These are awesome verses. I hope that you will meditate on them.

Many have stated that reading the book of Romans is the most rewarding experience in the Christian life, and I agree. To me, this book challenges one's thought processes, even though it seems philosophical at first. Then, as it settles in your heart, you realize that you are on holy ground, and it waters your soul like an oasis in a dry and thirsty land.

This epistle is the greatest document on our Salvation, for it will ground the believer in *the faith*. It is a personal letter, written for every believer. It is the Constitution of the Christian Faith.

An understanding of Romans requires all the mental ability that we have, and our study of it must be bathed in prayer and supplication before the Holy Spirit can teach us.

**Outline:**

1. *Doctrinal* – Romans 1-8: "Faith": The justification of the sinner, the revelation of the sin of man, and the revelation of the righteousness of God.

2. *Dispensational* – Romans 9-11: "Hope": God's past dealings with Israel; God's present dealings with Israel; God's future dealings with Israel.

3. *Duty* – Romans 12-16: "Love": The service of the believer. The separation of the believer.

In the Book of Romans, man's problem is identified, God's righteousness is revealed, and God's love is manifested in the Person of Jesus Christ. Glorious!!

## THE LETTERS OF FIRST & SECOND CORINTHIANS

**Author:** *The Apostle Paul*

**Date:** *c. AD 57*

**Place:** *written from Ephesus*

**Theme:** *The Lordship of Jesus (1 Corinthians 1:2-3, 7-8)*

**Background:**

Corinth was the "sin city" of the Roman Empire in Paul's day. It was the early equivalent of Vanity Fair. Located about 40 miles west of Athens on a narrow Isthmus between Peloponnesus and the mainland, Corinth was the great commercial center of the Roman Empire with three harbors, of which two were important: Lechaeum, about 1.5 miles to the West and Cenchreae about 8.5 miles to the East.

**Important dates:**

- 196 BC: Rome declared Corinth a free city.
- 146 BC: Corinth rebelled and was totally destroyed by Mummius, the Consul.
- 46 BC: Julius Caesar rebuilt it with great elegance, restoring it to its former prominence.

The temple of Aphrodite, built on the Acrocorinthus, was attended by 1,000 priestesses of vice. They were actually nothing more than prostitutes. The city was given over to licentiousness and pleasure. The Isthmian games were conducted here.

Against this corrupt background, Paul preached the gospel in Corinth, founded the church, and wrote two epistles, 1 and 2 Corinthians, to the believers there. Read Acts 18:1-18 for the account of Paul's visit to Corinth.

## THE FIRST LETTER TO THE CORINTHIANS

Paul wrote this letter in response to a letter from the church of Corinth that had been addressed to him. He wanted to discuss some issues that the church was having. It is a letter intended for the correction of errors and confirmation of Truth.

**Outline:**

1.  Salutation and thanksgiving, chapter 1:1-9

2.  Concerning conditions in the Corinthian church, chapters 1:10 – 16:9.

    Paul denounces sectarianism and divisions within the church and calls believers to be of one body in mind and heart. He speaks of the Centrality of Christ crucified, corrects divisions, clarifies the importance of paying attention to the Holy Spirit, corrects human wisdom, describes what Christian conduct is, explains the conditions of Christian servants, and urges Christian conduct. He explains the benefits and the power of the Holy Spirit.

    The church at Corinth was enjoying the power and benefits of the Spirit, but the experience had become carnal, and the people were puffed up. Paul explains how they ought to function in the Spirit in an orderly manner, because the basis of the Christian life is LOVE. Chapter 13 is known as the "Love Chapter." In chapter 15, Paul especially deals with the Risen Christ as "faith's reality"; The Risen Christ is "our Hope"; the last enemy destroyed is "Death." He warns of the effects of denying the Resurrection, explaining that the hope of Christian faith is actually in the Resurrection. Please meditate on chapter 15:12-19. It is very powerful!

God, who calls us to have fellowship with Him, to be His children, has also called us to be saints "set apart for His Holy use," and invites us into friendship with Him. Glorious!

3. Closing exhortation and benediction, chapter 16:10-24. My favorite verses are 16:13-14: "Watch, stand fast in the faith, be brave, be strong; let all that you do be done with LOVE."

*Amen.*

## THE SECOND LETTER TO THE CORINTHIANS

Shortly after Paul had written 1 Corinthians from Ephesus, where he was in grave danger (2 Corinthians 1:8), he wrote 2 Corinthians from Philippi. Paul was in Ephesus for approximately three years. He had sent Titus to Corinth because he could not personally go there at the time.

Timothy was with Paul in Ephesus, and these two proceeded to Troas to wait for Titus to bring word from Corinth (2 Corinthians 2:12-13). When Titus did not come, Paul and Timothy went on to Philippi, where Titus brought good news from the Corinthian church (2 Corinthians 7:5-11). Any breach between Paul and the Corinthian church was healed.

1. 1 Corinthians deals with the condition of and correction in the church.

2. 2 Corinthians deals with the condition of the ministry within the church.

**Outline:**

1.  The Comfort of God, chapters 1-7: "Christian living"

2.  The Collection for the poor saints at Jerusalem, chapters 8-9: "Christian giving"

3.  The Calling of the Apostle Paul, chapters 10-13: "Christian guarding"

**My favorite verses:** *2 Corinthians 5:17, 2 Corinthians 4:6*

---

*Therefore if anyone is in Christ, he is a new creation; old things have passed away; behold all things have become new. ~ For it is the God who commanded light to shine out of darkness (creation) who has shone in our hearts to give the light of the knowledge of the glory of God in the face of Jesus Christ. (KJV)*

---

## THE LETTER TO THE GALATIANS

**Author:** *The Apostle Paul*

**Date:** *c. AD 57*

This epistle is a stern, serious, and solemn message (see Galatians 1:6-9 and 3:1-5). It does not correct conduct, as the Corinthian letters did, but it is still corrective. The Galatian believers were in grave peril. Because the foundations of their faith were being attacked, everything was threatened.

This letter ("epistle") contains no word of commendation, praise, or thanksgiving. There is no request for prayer, and there is no mention of their standing in Christ. No one with Paul is mentioned by name (Galatians 1:2), being referred to merely as "all the brethren that are with me." Compare this with Paul's other letters.

In this letter, the heart of Paul the apostle is laid bare. You will sense his deep emotion and strong feeling. This is his "fighting letter." He has no tolerance for legalism. In this heartfelt letter, Paul challenges the foundation of their belief. This letter represents the declaration of emancipation from legalism of any kind. It is the manifesto of Christian liberty and the strongest declaration and defense of the doctrine of justification by faith. Not only is the sinner saved by grace through faith, but the saved sinner is *kept* and *lives* by grace.

*Meditate on Galatians 3:1-9

**Outline:**

1. Introduction, chapter 1:1-10

    - a. Personal authority of the apostle and the glory of the gospel, chapters 1:11- 2:14

    - b. The experience of Paul in Arabia, then with the apostles in Jerusalem, and in Antioch with Peter

2. Doctrinal "justification by faith," chapters 2:15-4:31: Faith vs. Works; Liberty vs. Bondage

3. Practical "santification by the Spirit," chapters 5:1-6:10: Spirit vs. Flesh; Liberty vs. bondage

4. Autographed conclusion, chapter 6:11-18.

    - a. The Cross of Christ vs. circumcision.

    - b. Christ's handwriting on Paul's "heart" represents the new circumcision of the new creation.

**Key verses:** *Galatians 2:19-21*

> *For I through the law am dead to the law, that I might live unto*
> *God. I am crucified with Christ: nevertheless I live; yet not I, but*
> *Christ liveth in me: and the life which I now live in the flesh I live*
> *by the faith of the Son of God, who loved me, and gave himself for*
> *me. I do not frustrate the grace of God: for if righteousness come*
> *by the law, then Christ is dead in vain.*

The difference of law and grace is clearly explained. The Law kills and Grace gives Life. Awesome!

## THE PRISON EPISTLES OF PAUL
### *Ephesians, Colossians, Philippians, Philemon*

THE PRISON EPISTLES were written by the Apostle Paul while he was in a Roman prison waiting for his day in court before Nero, the Caesar at the time, to whom Paul, as a Roman citizen, had appealed his case.

A quartet of men left Rome in the year AD 62, bound for the province of Asia Minor (Turkey and surrounding area). These four men held in their purses four of the most sublime compositions of the Christian faith. Rome's leaders did not comprehend the value and the significance of these writings of an unknown prisoner. If they had, these men would have been captured and the documents seized. When they bid farewell to the Apostle Paul, each was given a letter by Paul to bear to his particular constituency.

The four men who carried the letters were:

1.  *Tychicus from Ephesus* (Ephesians 6:21), who carried the letter to the Ephesians

2.  *Epaphroditus from Philippi* (Philippians 4:18), who took the letter to the Philippians

3.  *Epaphras from Colosse* (Colossians 4:12), who brought the letter to the Colossians

4.  *Onesimus, a slave from Colosse* (Philemon 10), who carried the letter from Paul to Philemon, his master.

These letters present a composite picture of Christ, the church, the life, and the interrelationship and functioning of all. These different facets present the Christian life on the highest plane.

- **Ephesians** presents "the church, which is His body" – this is the invisible church, of which Christ is the head. The church is seated with Christ.
- **Colossians** presents Christ, "the head of the body, the church," with the emphasis upon Christ, rather than on the church.
- **Philippians** presents Christian living with Christ as the dynamic: "I can do all things through Christ which strengthens me" (Philippians 4:13).
- **Philemon** represents Christian living in action in a pagan society: "If therefore you count me as a partner, receive him as myself and if he wronged you or owe anything put that on my account" (Philemon 17-18). The gospel walked in shoe leather in the first century church. It worked.

**Additionally:**

- In **Ephesians,** the church is God's masterpiece (Ephesians 2:10).
- In **Colossians**, Christ is the fullness of God. **Christ** is the theme (Colossians 2:9-10).
- In **Philippians,** Christ is the humble servant (Philippians 2:5-8).
- In **Philemon** the love of Christ binds a slave and master together. They become brothers in Christ.

## THE LETTER TO THE EPHESIANS

**Author:** *The Apostle Paul*

**Date:** *c. AD 62*

Paul arrived in Rome in AD 61 as a prisoner, and for two years he lived under house arrest, where he was permitted to receive visitors (Acts 28:16-30).

**Theme:** *The church as God's masterpiece*

This letter showcases the church as God's masterpiece (Ephesians 2:10). It is a mystery not revealed in the Old Testament. It is more wonderful than any temple made with hands, being constructed with living stones indwelt by the Holy Spirit (Ephesians 2: 20-22). It is the body of Christ, living in this world to walk as He would have walked and to wrestle against the wiles of the devil (1:22, 4:1, and 6:11-12). The temple of Diana, which was one of the seven wonders of the ancient world, was in Ephesus.

The church is far superior to the temple made with hands. The church is the body of Christ.

**Important Concepts:**

- God the Father planned the church (Ephesians 1:3-6)
- God the Son paid the price for the church (Ephesians 1:7-12)
- God the Holy Spirit protects the church (Ephesians 1:13-14)

**Outline 1:** *Doctrinal*

The heavenly calling of the church displays what we have in Christ. In chapters 1-3: We are placed in the higher planes in heaven inasmuch as we are actually seated with Christ in spiritual realms. As far as our Lord is concerned, we have already arrived and are in Heaven with Christ. We have everything we need, spiritually speaking. *The church* is not promised material blessings or given a particular land. But its members are "coheirs of the earth with Christ." In other words, the winner takes all!

Ephesians 2:4-10: The first three chapters present the position of the church, and the last three chapters describe how a church that is placed with Christ is to behave in the daily grind of everyday living in a corrupt world.

**Outline 2:** *Practical*

So now that we are in Christ, how are we to live? The earthly conduct of the church: We think and behave like kings and work like servants (Ephesians 4-6). We are to walk in love, walk in unity, walk in light, walk in wisdom. With these we defeat Satan in the Spirit.

**My favorite verses:**

- Ephesians 1:17-19: Paul's prayer for us
- Ephesians 2:10: We are His poem.
- Ephesians 2:15-18: Jews and Gentiles become one flesh, "the body of Christ, which is the church."

## THE LETTER TO THE PHILIPPIANS

"THE EARTHLY WALK OF HEAVENLY PEOPLE"

**Author:** *The Apostle Paul*

**Date:** *AD 62*

**Remarks:**

Philippi was a Roman colony, and the church of Philippi was less Jewish and more Gentile than were all the others. This was the first church established in Europe (Acts 16:6-40) in which the Gentiles had special position in the economy of God.

Women occupied a prominent place in this church. Paul's first meeting with the Philippians was not in a synagogue but at a prayer meeting of women (Acts 16:10-16). A woman named Lydia was the first convert in Europe. Two women were prominent in this church (Philippians 4:2), and there were others named who also labored in the church (4:3).

**Occasion for Paul's letter:**

The church at Philippi kept in close touch with the Apostle Paul (Philippians 4:15) but lost track of him when he was arrested in Jerusalem, and for two years there was no communication. Finally, they heard that he was in prison in Rome and immediately dispatched Pastor Epaphroditus to Rome with words of sympathy, a gift, and many expressions of love. Later, Epaphroditus fell ill in Rome. After he had recovered, Paul wrote this letter and sent it by the messenger who had also brought him assistance.

Two women who were prominent in the church were having some disagreement, and Paul was admonishing the church to help these women to be of same mind in the Lord. But this letter is also intended for exhortation and encouragement by the beloved Apostle Paul. It is a very practical letter.

**Key thought:** *Joy*

It has also been labeled "the secret of joy." Some form of the word occurs 19 times. It explains how a person may have joy in their heart even in a world that is ever changing, and its troubles are many. The person who is answering this question is in the Mamertine Prison in Rome. *Our joy does not depend on circumstance.*

**Outline:**

1.  Philosophy for Christian living, chapter 1 (Key verses 21-30)

2.  Pattern for Christian living, chapter 2 (Key verses 5-11)

3.  Price for Christian living, chapter 3 (Key verses 10-14)

4.  Power for Christian living, chapter 4 (Key verse 13)

This is Radical Christianity. The letter to the Philippians is one of my favorite books.

> J:    *Jesus.*
> O:    *Others.*
> Y:    *You. I am the third.*

*Shalom!*

## THE LETTER TO THE COLOSSIANS

**Author:** *The Apostle Paul*

**Date:** *AD 62*

**Background:**

Paul had never been to Colossae. He was in Ephesus for about two years during which time he had his most fruitful ministry (Acts 19:8-20). Colossae was 75-100 miles east of Ephesus. Visitors from Colossae had heard Paul's teaching and had come to know Christ. Philemon was apparently one of these converts. Thus the Colossian church came into existence (Philemon 1:2). Paul intended to visit there when he was released from prison (Philemon 1:22).

Paul wrote to this church as though it were his own. Epaphras was the pastor of that fellowship. The church's primary problem was Gnosticism, which had made its way into the church. What did this mean?

- They developed an exclusive spirit – they "were aristocratic in wisdom." Paul answers in 1:28.

- They held speculative tenets on creation, such as the idea that God did not create the universe but created a *creature* that in turn created the universe. Paul answers in 1:15-19 and 2:18.

- Their ethical practices were influenced by Asceticism (i.e., influenced by Greek Stoicism and unrestricted licentiousness from Greek Epicureanism). Paul answers in 2:16-23 and 3:5-9.

**Message of Colossians:**

Christ is the theme in this letter. Christianity lives between two ever-present dangers:

1. It might evaporate into philosophy. (But Christ is the answer to philosophy—Colossians 1:1-15. This message is for the head).

2. This teaching might become a formula. (Christ is the answer to ritualistic acts—Colossians 2:16-23. This message is for the heart).

In fact, neither philosophy nor ritual is correct. Jesus said that He is the *water* of life – not ice or steam. By this we mean that we ought not to add or subtract from Christ.

**Outline:**

1. Doctrinal (Colossians 1-2): Christ, the fullness of God

2. Practical (Colossians 3-4): Christ, The fullness of God poured out in life through believers

**Special features:**

- Pre-eminence of Christ (Colossians 1: 9-18)
- Reconciled with Christ (Colossians 1:19-23)
- Not philosophy but Christ (Colossians 2: 3-9)
- Not legalism but Christ (Colossians 2:13-14)
- Not carnality but Christ (Colossians 3:1-4)
- Character of the new man (Colossians 3:12-23 and 4:2-6)

The beauty, power, and Majesty of Christ is portrayed in this Letter.

*Peace.*

*[Note: Philemon is Paul's fourth Prison Epistle, but it appears canonically after Titus (see page 174).]*

# THE THESSALONIAN EPISTLES
*First & Second Thessalonians*

## THE FIRST LETTER TO THE THESSALONIANS

**Location:** *Thessalonica*

Thessalonica (modern-day Salonika) was a Roman colony and very important in the times of the Roman Empire. It was located about 50 miles west of Philippi and about 200 miles north of Athens. It was first named Therma because of the hot springs in the area. In 316 BC, Cassander—who succeeded Alexander the Great—named it in memory of his wife, Thessalonica. The church in Thessalonica was a model church. Paul cited it in his letter to the Corinthians as an example (1 Thessalonians 1:7 and 2 Corinthians 8:1-5). It was a poor church, but rich in Christ. The people shared out of their poverty.

**Occasion:**

This was the earliest letter written by Paul. It was written from Athens or Corinth on his second missionary journey. Paul had to leave Thessalonica due to great opposition to the Gospel. The enemy pursued him to Berea, and again Paul was forced to leave. He left Silas and Timothy at Berea, but he himself went on to Athens. It was there that Timothy brought him word from the church of Thessalonica (1 Thessalonians 3:6), together with some questions that they had raised. Paul then wrote the first letter in response to their overture.

**Theme:**

Waiting for the Second Coming of Christ for the believers before He returns to judge the world.

**Purpose:**

- To admonish believers to serve and to wait
- To confirm young converts in the elementary truth of the gospel
- To condition them that they must live for Christ (holy living)
- To comfort them regarding the return of Christ

A heathen inscription in Thessalonica read, "After death, no reviving. After the grave, no meeting again." Paul argues: "Not so for the believers in Christ. We shall live again because Christ lives."

**Outline:**

1. The Coming of Christ is an *inspiring hope* (chapter 1)
2. The Coming of Christ is a *working hope* (chapter 2)
3. The Coming of Christ is a *purifying hope* (chapters 3:1–4:12)
4. The Coming of Christ is a *comforting hope* (chapter 4:13-18)
5. The Coming of Christ is a *rousing hope* (chapter 5)

This letter suggests that we need to guard our steps as we look up for the coming of Christ.

My favorite verses are 1 Thessalonians 5:11-28. You will be blessed, as was I.

*Shalom.*

# THE SECOND LETTER TO THE THESSALONIANS

**Author:** *The Apostle Paul*

**Date:** *c. AD 52-53*

**Remarks:**

The first letter to the Thessalonians had given rise to further questions, and Paul is attempting to answer these concerns in a second epistle, shortly thereafter.

There was circulating in Thessalonica church a letter or a report purported to have come from Paul that was inclined to disturb the Christians. This false report claimed that Christ had already come and gathered the church to Himself, and the world was therefore living under judgment of the Day of the Lord. Their present persecution seemed to confirm this false report. Paul attempts to allay their fears by stating definitely that our gathering together with the Lord is yet in the future.

**Theme:**

1. 1 Thessalonians talks about the return of Christ for the believers one day.

2. 2 Thessalonians talks about The Great Tribulation that will come upon the world some day—"The Day Of The Lord"

**Outline:**

1. Persecution of believers now and judgment of unbelievers thereafter at the coming of Christ (2 Thessalonians 1)

2. Program for the world in connection with the coming of Christ (2 Thessalonians 2)

3. Practicality of the coming of Christ (2 Thessalonians 2:13 to 3:18). Believers should be established in the Word. (2 Thessalonians 2:13-17):

   - In their walk (2 Thessalonians 3:1-7)
   - In their work (2 Thessalonians 3:8-18)

**My favorite passage:** *2 Thessalonians 1:10-12*

---

*. . . When He comes, in that Day, to be glorified in His saints and to be admired among all those who believe, because our testimony among you was believed. Therefore we also pray always for you that our God would count you worthy of this calling, and fulfill all the good pleasure of His goodness and the work of faith with power, that the name of our Lord Jesus Christ may be glorified in you, and you in Him, according to the grace of our God and the Lord Jesus Christ.*

---

*Peace.*

# THE PASTORIAL EPISTLES
*First & Second Timothy, and Titus*

THESE LETTERS are labeled the Pastoral Epistles. Paul writes these letters to his two young converts (1 Timothy 1:2; Titus 1:4) who had followed him on many of his missionary journeys and whom he had established as pastors of churches at the writing of these epistles. He gave instruction for the orderly procedures within the local and visible church.

These letters direct a particular message to young pastors and have pertinent instructions for the present-day church. Although they were addressed by Paul to his young friends in the ministry and not to the churches, the message is appropriate for the churches.

## THE FIRST LETTER TO TIMOTHY

**Author:** *The Apostle Paul*

**Date:** *c. AD 64*

**Theme:** *Government and order within the local church*

It is necessary to have government and order within the local church. This is in contrast to the letter to the Ephesians, where Paul explains that the church is the body of Christ, "the invisible church." This letter is addressed to an assembly of believers in a local church and organized for a common purpose.

**Key verses:** *1 Timothy 1:3, 3:15*

Sound doctrine and correct conduct identify the local church.

**Outline:**

1. The faith of the church (1 Timothy 1)

2. Public prayer and women's place within the church (1 Timothy 2)

3. Officers in the church (1 Timothy 3)

4. Apostasy in the church (1 Timothy 4)

5. Duties of officers in the church (1 Timothy 5-6)

   - The relationship of ministries to different groups within the local church (1 Timothy 5)

   - The relationship of believers to others (1 Timothy

The heart of Paul is seen as he works with this young, timid pastor. He addresses him as a son. He gives instructions for how believers of the local church operate in the day-to-day routines of life under Christ.

I love this letter because it describes the down-to-earth, practical life of believers operating under the Spirit. This letter is filled to the brim with the goodness of our Lord. Because of that, I found it difficult to choose a favorite verse. In the end, I simply could not pass over 1 Timothy 6:11-16. You will be blessed by these verses.

*Shalom.*

## THE SECOND LETTER TO TIMOTHY

**Author:** *The Apostle Paul*

**Date:** *c. AD 67*

It is believed that Paul wrote this letter just prior to his death.

**Key verses:** *2 Timothy 2:15 and 4:2*

**Key words:** *"Not ashamed" and "endure"*

**Theme:** *Loyalty in the days of apostasy*

- Loyalty in suffering, chapter 1
- Loyalty in service, chapter 2
- Loyalty in apostasy, chapter 3-4:5
- The Lord was loyal to His servants even when they deserted him, chapter 4:6-18

Apostasy is total desertion of faith due to deliberate error. It is intentional departure from the true faith (Luke 18:8). Although the visible church has entered the orbit of terrible apostasy, the invisible church is on its way to the Epiphany of Glory.

**Outline:**

1. Affliction of the Gospel (2 Timothy 1)

2. Active in service (2 Timothy 2)

3. Apostasy is coming; the authority of the scriptures (2 Timothy 3:1-4:5)

4. Allegiance to the Lord and of the Lord (2 Timothy 4:6-22)

   - The deathbed testimony of Paul (2 Timothy 4: 6-8)
   - Paul's last words (2 Timothy 4:9-22)

O the faithfulness of this apostle and the Lord! I had a difficult time separating them, for Paul and the Lord somehow mingled together and became one. I wept much studying this epistle. It is indeed the swan song of this beloved apostle.

## THE LETTER TO TITUS

**Author:** *The Apostle Paul*

**Date:** *AD 64-67 (see notes on 1 Timothy)*

**Remarks:**

While little is known of either Timothy or Titus, there seems to have quite a contrast between them. Titus appears to have been a stronger man, both physically and spiritually, since Paul expresses less concern for his welfare.

Titus was probably more mature and possessed a more virile personality. Timothy was a Jew who had been circumcised by Paul, but Titus was a Gentile. Paul seems to have refused to circumcise him (Galatians 2:3) because in Christ "neither circumcision nor uncircumcision [has a value] but a new creation" (Galatians 6:15).

**Theme:** *The return of Christ (Titus 2:13)*

Here is a good picture of the New Testament Church in its well-rounded representation in the community as an organization, showing that it should be orderly, sound in doctrine, pure in life, and ready to do every good work.

**Outline:**

1.  The church is an organization (Titus 1)

2.  The church is to teach and preach the Word of God (Titus 2)

3.  The church is to perform good works (Titus 3, i.e., "the work of the Holy Spirit")

**Favorite passage:** *Titus 2:11-14*

---

*For the grace of God that bringeth salvation hath appeared to all men, Teaching us that, denying ungodliness and worldly lusts, we should live soberly, righteously, and godly, in this present world; Looking for that blessed hope, and the glorious appearing of the great God and our Saviour Jesus Christ; Who gave himself for us, that he might redeem us from all iniquity, and purify unto himself a peculiar people, zealous of good works.*

---

This concludes the Pastoral Epistles, which are for instruction and encouragement not only for pastors but also for believers everywhere.

*BLESSINGS.*

## THE LETTER TO PHILEMON

**Author:** *The Apostle Paul*

**Date:** *c. AD 62 (see outline of Ephesians, the prison Epistles introduction)*

Philemon is the fourth letter of the prison Epistles.

The Epistles present a different style in revelation. God used law, history, poetry, prophecy, and the gospels up until this point. But in the Epistles, God adopted a more personal and direct method. In this intimate way, He looks to the cross and talks about the church.

Some have said that the Epistles are love letters from Christ to His church. (I agree.)

The Epistle of Philemon is individual and intimate. There is reason to believe that Paul did not expect its contents to be revealed to the public. At other times he knew that what he was writing was

Scripture. This does not detract from the inspiration and value of Philemon but rather enhances its message.

**Background:**

The story behind this letter to Philemon was acted out on the black background of slavery. There were approximately 60 million slaves in the Roman Empire, where the total population did not exeed 120 million. A slave was simply chattel. A slave was treated as well or as poorly as his master wished. Slaves had no rights themselves and no courts to which they could appeal.

Onesimus was a slave belonging to Philemon, a Christian of Colossae. This slave, Onesimus, was a runaway slave to Rome and found himself where Paul was preaching. When he heard the gospel of Jesus Christ, the Holy Spirit regenerated him, making him a new creature in Christ. He told his story to Paul, and Paul sent him back to Philemon with an accompanying letter.

**Purpose:**

The primary purpose of this letter is to reveal Christ's love for us in pleading our case before God. The finest illustration of substitutionary atonement is when Paul wrote to Philemon stating," If he wronged you or owes you anything, put it on my account" (verse 18). We can hear Christ agreeing to take our place and to have all of our sins imputed to Him, for "He made Him who knew no sin to be a sin for us" (2 Corinthians 5:21). He took our place in His death, but He gave us His place in life. Paul says, "If then you count me as partner, receive him as you would me," (Philemon 17). We either have the standing of Christ before God or we have no standing at all. He took our hell and gave us His heaven that "we might be made the righteousness of God in Him" (2 Corinthians 5:21).

Onesimus, an unprofitable runaway slave, was to be received as Paul the Apostle himself. The great apostle would have been received in the home of Philemon. The practical purpose of this book is to teach brotherly love. Paul spoke of the new relationship between master and servant in the other prison epistles. Here he demonstrates how it should work. These two men, belonging to two different classes in the Roman Empire (which often hated or mistreated each other) are now brothers in Christ, and they are to act like it. This is the only solution to the problem of capital and labor. This indeed is a radical Christianity!

**Favorite verse:** *1:17-18*

> *If then you count me as a partner, receive him as you would me. But if he has wronged you or owes anything, put that on my account.*

*I love this book! Shalom.*

# THE GENERAL EPISTLES
*Hebrews, James, 1&2 Peter, 1/2/3 John, Jude*

## THE LETTER TO THE HEBREWS

**Author:** *Unknown, but many believe it may have been the Apostle Paul*

**Date:** *Before the destruction of the Temple in AD 70*

This is one of my favorite books. Some have said that the Book of Romans reveals the *necessity* of the Christian faith while Hebrews reveals the *superiority* of the Christian faith.

**Notes:** *The Law is Good, Grace is Better, Glory is Best*

The comparative word "better" occurs 13 times.

**Subject:** *The superiority of Christ*

**Outline 1:** *Christ is better than the Old Testament economy (Hebrews 1-10).*

- A: Christ is superior to the prophets (Hebrews 1:1-3)
- B: Christ is superior to the angels (Hebrews 1:4-2:18)
- C: Christ is superior to Moses (Hebrews 3:1-4:2)
- D: Christ is superior to Joshua (Hebrews 4:3-13)
- E: Christ is superior to the Levitical priesthood (Hebrews 4:14-7:28). Christ our high priest is after the order of Melchizedek. Christ is a Priest perpetually (Hebrews 7:4-22). Christ *in His person* is perpetual and perfect Priest (Hebrews 7:23-28). Christ as our high priest ministers in a superior sanctuary by a better covenant built upon better promises (Hebrews 8:1-10:39).

**Outline 2:** *Christ brings better benefits and duties (Hebrews 11-13: The practical aspects of the book)*

A: FAITH: Hebrews 11:1-40
(The secret life of believers—13:1-6)
B: HOPE: Hebrews 12:1-29
(The social life of believers—13:7-14)
C: LOVE: Hebrews 13:1-25
(The spiritual life of believers—13:15-19)

**Outline 3:** *Special and personal benediction (Hebrews 13:20-25)*

This book is rich. I had difficulty choosing a favorite verse. So many books of the Old Testament are quoted here, especially the book of Psalms.

But I will settle on Hebrews 12:2: "…looking unto Jesus, the author and finisher of our faith, who for the joy that was set before Him endured the cross, despising the shame, and has sat down at the right hand of the throne of God."

*Blessings.*

## THE EPISTLE OF JAMES

James 1 and 2 Peter—as well as 1, 2, and 3 John and Jude—are designated as "catholic" epistles in the sense of "universal" because they are not addressed to a particular individual or church, but to the church as a whole.

**Author:** *James*

Date: c. AD 45 and believed to be the first book of the New Testament to be written. James was the half-brother of the Lord Jesus (Matthew 13:55). He came to faith after the resurrection and became head of the church in Jerusalem.

As a young believer, I had difficulty understanding this book and got the impression that one must do works in order to keep one's faith in Christ. Because it is practical book on the Christian duty, it is easy for the new believer to assume that he or she must work for their faith. That is why I am hesitant to point the new believer to the book of James before they establish their identity in Christ.

The Apostle Paul says, "You are justified by faith." The Apostle James says, "Justification by faith is demonstrated by works." This seeming contradiction between these apostles can be easily explained when the message of James is considered.

James takes the position, as Paul does, that we are justified by faith, but that the faith that justifies produces good works. Faith alone saves, but the faith that saves is not alone. Justification is shown by works and we are not justified by but for good works.

James and Paul present the two aspects of Justification by Faith. Paul emphasized both phases:

- Faith: We are not justified *by* works (Ephesians 2:8, Titus 3:5)

- Works: We are justified *for* works (Titus 3:8, Ephesians 2:10). Faith is the *root* of salvation; works are the *fruit* of salvation. Faith is the *cause* of salvation, while works are the *result* of salvation.

When James talks about works, he is talking about the fruit of the Spirit.

**Key verses:** *James 1:22 & 2:20*

**Theme:** *The practical daily life of the believer*

The "ethics of Christianity" do not equal Doctrine. This epistle is compared to the book of Proverbs in the Old Testament. Both the book of James and the book of Proverbs emphasize the practical daily life of the believer during which the faith of the child of God is tested.

**Outline:**

1. The *verification* of genuine faith (James 1-3—"What is in the well of the heart will come up through the bucket of the mouth.")

2. The *vacuity and vapidness* of worldliness (James 4—"Worldliness is identified with fighting and the spirit of dissension.")

3. The *vexation* of the rich. The *value* of the imminent coming of Christ, chapter 5. *The soon coming of Christ produces patience)*

Justification by faith is demonstrated by works.

1. *Works:* James 1-2

2. *Words:* James 3

3. *Worldliness:* James 4

4. *Warning to the rich:* James 5

*Shalom.*

## THE EPISTLE OF 1 PETER

**Author:** *Simon Peter*

Peter has been called "the ignorant fisherman," but no man who had spent three years in the school of Jesus could be called ignorant, and the epistles of Peter confirm this.

**Date:** *c. AD 64-67*

Peter wrote his two epistles and was put to death sometime during this period.

**Location:**

Believed to be Babylon (1 Peter 5:13). There is no evidence that he was in Rome. There was at this time a large Jewish colony in ancient Babylon that had fled Rome due to severe persecution under Claudius, and during the time of writing this epistle, bloody Nero was on the throne. This is in harmony with the theme of this letter.

**Theme:**

Christian hope in the time of trial. Peter immediately introduces the Trinity in 1 Peter 1:2. Peter is called the apostle of *hope*. Paul is called the apostle of *faith*. John is called the apostle of *love*.

**Key word:** *Knowledge*

**Outline:**

1. The suffering and the security of the believer produces joy (1 Peter 1:1-9).

2. The suffering and the studying of the Scriptures by believers produces holiness (1 Peter 1:10-25).

3. The suffering and also understanding the suffering of Christ produces separation, holy conduct, and obedience to the will of God (1 Peter 2-4).

4. The suffering and the awareness of the Second Coming of Christ by the believer produces a willingness to serve and to hope. They also produce humility and patience (1 Peter 5).

Here we see that Peter is not impetuous as before, but he is now patient and tender. The transforming power of the gospel had wrought this change in his life. I wholeheartedly suggest that you camp in this epistle for a while!

**Favorite passage:** *1 Peter 2:9-10*

---

*But you are a chosen generation, a royal priesthood, a holy nation, His own special people, that you may proclaim the praises of Him who called you out of darkness into His marvelous light; who once were not a people but are now the people of God, who had not obtained mercy but now have obtained mercy.*

---

*Blessings.*

<h2>THE EPISTLE OF 2 PETER</h2>

**Author:** *Peter (1:1)*

**Date:** *c. AD 66*

This second epistle was written shortly after the first epistle (2 Peter 3:1) and a short while before his martyrdom (2 Peter 1:13-14).

**Theme:** *Peter warns of heresy among the teachers*

This letter is the swan song of Peter as 2 Timothy is the swan song of Paul. There is a striking similarity: both epistles put up a warning sign along the Pilgrim's Pathway that the church is traveling, identifying the apostasy that was heading their way at the time and now, in our time, has arrived. Peter warns of heresy among the teachers as Paul warns of heresy among the laity. Both Peter and Paul speak in a joyful manner of their approaching deaths (2 Peter 1:13-14 and 2 Timothy 4:6-8). Both apostles anchor the church on the Scripture as the only defense against the coming apostasy.

**Key word:** *Knowledge (2 Peter 3:18)*

True knowledge, as opposed to gnosticism, is not some esoteric information concerning a form or formula, rite or ritual, nor is it some secret order or password. It is to know Jesus Christ as He is revealed to man in the Word of God. This is the secret to life and Christian living.

**Key passage:** *2 Peter 1:16-21*

---

*For we did not follow cunningly devised fables when we made known to you the power and coming of our Lord Jesus Christ, but were eyewitnesses of His majesty. For He received from God the Father honor and glory when such a voice came to Him from the Excellent Glory: "This is My beloved Son, in whom I am well pleased." And we heard this voice which came from heaven when we were with Him on the holy mountain. And so we have the prophetic word confirmed, which you do well to heed as a light that shines in a dark place, until the day dawns and the morning star rises in your hearts; knowing this first, that no prophecy of Scripture is of any private interpretation, for prophecy never came by the will of man, but holy men of God spoke as they were moved by the Holy Spirit.*

---

So rich! Please meditate on these verses, which describe the trustworthy prophetic Word.

**Outline:**

1. The Addition of Christian graces gives assurance (2 Peter 1:1-14): The full knowledge of God and of Jesus Christ our Lord is the foundation on which Christian character is built.

2. The Authority of the Scripture is attested to by fulfilled prophecy (2 Peter 1:15- 21). The Scriptures give light for obedience in dark days.

3. Apostasy was brought in by false teachers (2 Peter 2). The church must be aware of false teachers.

4. Attitudes toward the return of the Lord are a test of apostasy (2 Peter 3:1-4).

5. Agenda of God for the world—past, present, and future (2 Peter 3:5-13).

6. Admonition to believers (2 Peter 3:14-18). Keep in mind that knowledge of God's program is an incentive to grow in the knowledge of our Lord and Savior Jesus Christ.

**Favorite verse:** *2 Peter 3:18*

*But grow in the grace and knowledge of our Lord and Savior Jesus Christ. To Him be Glory both now and forever, Amen.*

*Peace.*

## THE EPISTLE OF 1 JOHN

**Author:** *The Apostle John*

John evidently wrote his gospel first, then his epistles, and finally, the book of Revelation before his death about AD 100.

**Theme:** *Love can only be expressed in the boundary of Truth*

**Purpose:**

John expressed the purpose for his writing in each of the three types of revelation. In the Gospel of John, the reason for writing is stated in John 20:30-31. Also in 1 John 5:13; in Revelation 1:19.

The fivefold purpose for John writing this epistle:

1. Fellowship with God, the Lord Jesus, and with one another (1 John 1:3)

2. That our joy maybe full (1 John 1:4)

3. That we may not sin (1 John 2:1-2)

4. That we may know we have eternal life (John 5:13)

5. That we may believe on the name of the Son of God, *JESUS*."

This epistle takes the child of God across the threshold into the fellowship of our Father's home. It is a family letter; John is writing to the family of God. Paul wrote to the church. John wrote to the family. The *church* is a body of believers in the position where they are "blessed with all spiritual blessings in the heavenlies in Christ" (Ephesians 1:3). We are given this position when we receive the Lord Jesus. In the *family*, we have relationships that can be thwarted but restored when we admit that we have offended a Holy God and apologize to Him (1 John 1:9). Restoration is a family affair—not salvation but fellowship, e.g., the story of the prodigal son (Luke 15:11-23).

John wrote this epistle to counter the first heresy that had entered the church. It was Gnosticism—an aberrant belief which boasted superior knowledge of spiritual matters (Gnosis). The Gnostics accepted the deity of Jesus, but denied His Humanity. By contrast, John gives us the true Ginosko—or knowledge of God's Son. The "disciple whom Jesus loved" used this Greek word for "intimate knowledge" or "complete understanding" more than any other New Testament contributor—including 49 times in his gospel, 21 times in his first epistle, and once in his second.

**Outline:**

1. *God is Light,* v. 1:5 (see also 1 John 1:1-2:2

2. *God is Love,* v. 4:8 (1 John 2:3-4:21)

3. *God is Life,* v. 5:12 (1 John 5)

**Keywords:** *LIGHT, LOVE, LIFE*

*Amen.*

## THE EPISTLE OF 2 JOHN

**Author:** *The Apostle John*

**Date:** *c. AD 90-100*

This is a personal letter written to a particular lady or a local church that was extending hospitality to all those who claimed to be Christian, although some were heretics. John is warning them.

**Theme:** *Truth is worth standing for*

Truth is worth contending for, and it is wrong to receive false teachers.

**Outline:**

1. Love expressed in the boundary of truth: 2 John 1-6. "Love in truth."

2. Life is an expression of the doctrine of Christ: 2 John 7-11. "False doctrine leads to evil deeds."

3. Personal greeting: 2 John 12-13. "False teachers are not to be received by Christians, but true teachers are to be received with joy."

## THE EPISTLE OF 3 JOHN

**Author:** *The Apostle John*

**Date:** *AD 90-100*

**Theme:** *Truth is worth working for*

This letter is similar to John's second letter in that it is personal in character and carries the same theme of truth.

**Outline:**

1. Gaius, beloved brother in the early church (3 John 1-8). Here John is urging Gaius to extend hospitality to true teachers of the word (v.2).

2. Diotrephes, "who loves to have the pre-eminence" (vv. 9-11). (Evil deeds are an expression of false doctrine.)

3. Demetrius had good report of all men, and of the truth itself verses (vv.12-14).

A good life is an expression of true Doctrine.

*Peace.*

## THE EPISTLE OF JUDE

**Author:** *Jude (brother of James and half-brother of the Lord Jesus)*

**Date:** *c. A.D 66-69*

**Theme:** *Assurance in the day of apostasy*

**Remarks:**

Jude was intending to write an epistle regarding our common salvation when the Spirit detoured him concerning the apostasy. It is a graphic and striking description that what was a little cloud, in Jude's day, is in our day a storm of hurricane proportions because we are in the apostasy, of which Jude foretold. It is a question now of how much worse it can get before the end comes.

Even though Jude is only one chapter, it is loaded with amazing truths about God, His word, faith, and spiritual man verses natural man. Jude gives the only record in Scripture of the contention over the body of Moses. Also, only Jude gives the prophecy of Enoch. Jude affords a fitting introduction to the book of Revelation.

**Outline:**

1. *Occasion of the epistle* (vv. 1-3) - Assurance for believers who are sanctified, kept, and called. The theme then changes to apostasy

2. *Occurrences of apostasy* (vv. 4-16):
   - The inception of apostasy
   - Israel in the wilderness in unbelief was destroyed
   - Angels rebelled and then were kept in chains
   - Sodom and Gomorrah: the people were committing sexual sin and were destroyed

- Modern apostate teachers are identified as those who *despise authority*
- Cain, Balaam, Korah, are all examples of apostates
- Apostate teachers are defined and described

3. *The occupation of believers* in the days of apostasy (vv.17-25)

- Believers are warned by apostles that these apostate ones would come
- What believers must do in the days of apostasy: Build up one another, pray in faith, keep themselves from sin, look for and have compassion on others, save others, hate evil

*Amen.*

# chapter fifteen

# Prophecy in the New Testament

## THE BOOK OF REVELATION

**Author:** *The Apostle John*

**Date:** *c. AD 95*

**Theme:**

Note that the title of this book is "Revelation," not "Revelations." While there are many fascinating prophetic events revealed in this book, its purpose and primary theme is the *singular* revelation, or "revealing," of Jesus Christ as King of Kings and Lord of Lords, who is the "kinsmen-redeemer" of all mankind, who alone is worthy to unseal the title deed to planet earth (Revelation 5:1-10).

**Remarks:**

This is the only purely prophetic book in the New Testament. In contrast to the 17 prophetic books in the Old Testament, the apostle

John reaches back into eternity *past* more than any other writer in Scripture in his Gospel of John 1:1-3. He now reaches farther into eternity *future* in the Book of Revelation.

Special blessings are promised to those who read, hear, and keep this book (Revelation 1:3). Likewise, a warning is issued to those who tamper with its contents (Revelation 22: 18-19). Revelation from God is not sealed (Revelation 22:10). Contrast Daniel 12:9—there it is a series of visions expressed in symbols.

**Outline:**

1.  *The Person of Christ:* Here John is instructed to "write the things which he has seen," i.e., "The Glorified Christ" (Revelation1:13-17).

2.  *The Possession of Jesus Christ:* The "church in the world" (Revelation 2-3). Jesus writes seven letters to seven churches to give them His appraisal. Here our Lord examines how well each one has lived the Christian life within the church as a whole and also as the individual Christian.

3.  *The Program of Jesus Christ:* The church in heaven and the Great Tribulation in the world. The believers are rewarded and those who turned their back on Jesus and refused to receive Him are judged according to their Deeds. This book is great news for the believer and a nightmare for the unbeliever. I shudder and tremble for them. I am thankful for the gift of God in forgiving my sin and restoring me to life.

Here I see two screenplays:

1. In heaven, there is celebration of continuous praise and worship at the Throne of God and the Lamb.

2. On earth, death and destruction reign. But here we also see the greatest harvest the world has ever had. More people come to Jesus than at any other period in the history of the world, which demonstrates God's loving kindness and mercy.

The book of Revelation is also a book of Blessings." Blessing means "favor with God," a state of happiness, completeness with contentment, God's favor upon our lives. As my pastor once said, "Our God is a blessing and compassionate God." So here in this book our God gives seven blessings, as pastor taught us:

1. Revelation 1:3: *Reading, hearing, and keeping the words of this book brings blessing.*

2. Revelation 14:13: *Blessed are believers who die in the Lord.*

3. Revelation 16:15: *Blessed are the ones who persevere and wait for the Lord.*

4. Revelation 19:9: *Blessed are they who are called to the marriage supper of the Lamb.*

5. Revelation 20:6: *Blessed are those of first Resurrection; over such the second death has no power.*

6. Revelation 22:7: *Blessed are those who keep the prophecies of this book.*

7. Revelation 22:14: *Blessed are those who do the commandments of this book.*

Our God is a blessing God, for our God is not willing that any should perish but that all would come to Him for life.

The book ends, or shall I say *begins*, with all things made new: the New Jerusalem, with all Her Glory, the River of Life; and the Tree of Life, which had disappeared in Genesis 3:22-24, appears once again. Thus man and God are reconciled once more! No more tears, no more pain, no more separation from Our God. As believers, we are reconnected the moment we receive our "Champion," THE LORD JESUS. GLORIOUS!!

*Blessings.*

# afterword

DEAR READER, Do you remember the incident that I had with my roommate while in Israel, which I mentioned in the beginning of this book and how I knew that the Lord wanted me to let it go?

I want to tell you that I did let go of it! I truly believed that I had moved on. But once in a while I found it surfacing again, and during those moments, I always sent a blessing her way, asking God to help me to truly not hold anything against her. God has His wonderful ways of answering our prayers. Here is what happened:

About a month ago, I came face to face with this woman, and I froze. I could not even return her "Hello." I was absolutely crushed, because I thought that I had moved on and had forgiven her—and I truly had! But I did not know the depths of my own wounded heart and that devastated me. I went home that night and wept bitterly.

All I could say was, "Lord I love You! Lord, I need you! My relationship with You is well, for I am forgiven and this is the 'vertical' part. But my relationship with my sister is not. It is 'horizontal,' and I am unable to see the Cross in that situation. I need You to heal me so that I can see the Cross in this relationship."

My friends, I have experienced a miracle!

That very night I felt the Love and Peace of Jesus and was comforted immensely. Last week at our women's retreat, we met again! I was so happy to see her, and I gave her my famous hug and kissed her. I did not want to let her go!

This is my Jesus, and this is why I wrote this book—so that the world might know and receive the love, forgiveness, and healing that only He can provide! I am so forever grateful for Him. I did not know my heart—but He knew my heart, for it is His abiding place! My heart needed to heal and to be mended.

Will you allow the Lord to work in your heart and soul and mind? He will if you let Him. This is my hope and prayer for each and every one of you—that your salvation and healing begins today.

For behold, He makes all things beautiful—in His time!

*In His grip,*

*Maryama Burger*
*sistermaryama.blogspot.com*

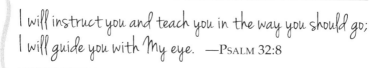

I will instruct you and teach you in the way you should go; I will guide you with My eye. —PSALM 32:8

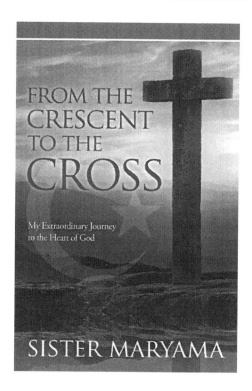

Made in the USA
San Bernardino, CA
07 March 2018